D1013145

PULL
IT OFF

PULL IT OFF

REMOVING YOUR FEARS AND PUTTING ON CONFIDENCE

Julianna Zobrist

New York   Nashville

Copyright © 2018 by Julianna Zobrist

Cover design by Lauren Hall. Cover photograph by Adam Jason Cohen. Cover copyright © 2018 by Hachette Book Group, Inc.

Hachette Book Group supports the right to free expression and the value of copyright. The purpose of copyright is to encourage writers and artists to produce the creative works that enrich our culture.

The scanning, uploading, and distribution of this book without permission is a theft of the author's intellectual property. If you would like permission to use material from the book (other than for review purposes), please contact permissions@hbgusa.com. Thank you for your support of the author's rights.

FaithWords
Hachette Book Group
1290 Avenue of the Americas, New York, NY 10104
faithwords.com
twitter.com/faithwords

First Edition: September 2018

FaithWords is a division of Hachette Book Group, Inc. The FaithWords name and logo are trademarks of Hachette Book Group, Inc.

The publisher is not responsible for websites (or their content) that are not owned by the publisher.

The Hachette Speakers Bureau provides a wide range of authors for speaking events. To find out more, go to www.hachettespeakersbureau.com or call (866) 376-6591.

Scriptures noted (NIV) are taken from the Holy Bible, New International Version®, NIV®. Copyright © 1973, 1978, 1984, 2011 by Biblica, Inc.™ Used by permission of Zondervan. All rights reserved worldwide. www.zondervan.com The "NIV" and "New International Version" are trademarks registered in the United States Patent and Trademark Office by Biblica, Inc.™

Scriptures noted (ESV) are from The ESV® Bible (The Holy Bible, English Standard Version®). ESV® Permanent Text Edition® (2016). Copyright © 2001 by Crossway, a publishing ministry of Good News Publishers. The ESV® text has been reproduced in cooperation with and by permission of Good News Publishers. Unauthorized reproduction of this publication is prohibited. All rights reserved.

Scriptures noted (NASB) are taken from the New American Standard Bible®, copyright © 1960, 1962, 1963, 1968, 1972, 1975, 1977, 1995 by The Lockman Foundation. Used by permission.

Scriptures noted (NLT) are taken from the Holy Bible, New Living Translation, copyright © 1996, 2004, 2007 by Tyndale House Foundation. Used by permission of Tyndale House Publishers, Inc., Carol Stream, Illinois 60188. All rights reserved.

Library of Congress Cataloging-in-Publication Data has been applied for.

ISBNs: 978-1-5460-2592-4 (hardcover), 978-1-5460-2594-8 (ebook), 978-1-5460-3514-5 (B&N Black Friday Signed Edition), 978-1-5460-3513-8 (BN.com Signed Edition)

Printed in the United States of America

LSC-C

10 9 8 7 6 5 4 3 2 1

*For Ben, Zion, Kruse, Blaise, and all
the Color Kids*

CONTENTS

PULL
IT OFF

WELCOME
AN INTRODUCTION
TO MY BRAIN

Anyone who follows me on social media knows I'm obsessed with my husband, Ben. Something about that baseball butt and kind heart just gets me every time. Sure, some days aren't so great and we bicker about the dumbest things, but most days (and the ones I choose to hold on to) feel easy and uncontrived. When it's just us, we aren't trying too hard and we're not overthinking the little things. When it's just us, we are not trying to make the other person someone they are not, and in turn, we are not putting pressure on our own selves to be something we aren't. When it's just us, it feels uncomplicated and sincere.

Ironically, the day when we decided to get hitched and make it "just us" forever felt like anything *but* that.

Those weeks leading up to the wedding should have been filled with days of excitement and anticipation. But, alas, they were filled with let's-get-this-over-with, can't-we-just-elope, don't-touch-me, you're-annoying days instead.

Planning an out-of-state wedding while taking twenty-one credits a semester for college was a little intense, so we occasionally dreamed of throwing the bird to the world and running away to Montana. To be honest, I'm not really sure why we selected that state—neither of us had been, and, in fact, we still haven't gone—but for some reason, it still seems ideal.

The big day for "just us" ended by being a day for everybody else and their dog-sitter's second cousin's mom.

The main characters in the actual wedding day were simply pawns—glorified party planners—given the task of throwing everyone in the universe a party that would be worth the plane flight and money it cost to buy the ugly bridesmaid dress. In fact, the bride and groom are virtually the last people a wedding day is for. Who cares if your favorite kind of cake is carrot? Someone *might* be allergic. Cancel the carrot. Who cares if you like pop jams blaring out on the dance floor? Someone *might* be offended by that kind of music. Cancel the DJ. Who cares if you just really, really love pink and want to wear a pink wedding dress? Someone *might* question the purity of your marriage. Go buy a white one, dummy.

Lest you think that I did not succumb to any of this nonsense, let me tell you something. I bought *two* wedding dresses. Two. I was so terrified by feeling sexy in dress number one that I took it back and bought dress number two.

It didn't stop there. I decided against the music I love to dance to because "Aunt Bertha" would complain it was too loud and aggressive (when her disappointment was truly because she wouldn't be able to hear all the gossip at the other end of the table). I decided to not do a champagne toast even though I think of champagne as basically a more enjoyable sparkling water. Why refuse the bubbly, you ask? Because someone *might* be offended. To be fair, no one had raised a concern, but I was worried that *maybe* in the sea of 400 faces who attended our wedding, there *might* just *maybe* be someone who would get miffed.

Talk about walking on eggshells. It's a miracle anyone ends up getting married at the end of an engagement, because death by engagement is probably a thing. Thank the good Lord for my mother, who made the wedding day come together seamlessly. She could legitimately run the world with her brains and fortitude.

Here's the thing about living to make everyone else around you happy: It will never happen.

That Disney princess fantasy you have in your head that everyone must like you and you must never offend anyone or piss anyone off? It's a fairy tale. That's right. Tooth Fairy, Easter Bunny, Atlantis, Santa Claus, Pleasing All of Humanity = Not Real Life.

So why do we live our lives as if the ability to please every living male and female at any given moment is even a possibility? How can we be people who are gracious and kind, not because we live in a bunker, but because we are confident and secure and unapologetic?

Good question.

We are humans in desperate need of the One who not only exposes the reality of who we are but also opens our eyes and lovingly makes us His. He changes the beat to our song; instead of hiding or trying to become something we cannot, we sing of our humanness. After all, He made us this way. When we know that, we can let our transparency and vulnerability take their appropriate role as the common ground between each of us. This knowledge of acceptance by God amidst vulnerability will be the soil out of which grows a confident, aware, and free person. The you of yous.

In this book, we are going to journey together through the question I get asked most often: How do you pull it off? While this question is usually in regard to the seemingly life-sized Crayola box I must surely have gotten dressed in that morning, this book is most *definitely* not about clothes, because your self-expression is only an outward display of the confidence you feel inside. However, this book is about the question that seems to probe most of modernity today: How can we be completely transparent and vulnerable with ourselves and others, and yet be secure and confident enough to walk through life without fear?

Pull It Off is broken down into three parts that will address the issues of authority, identity, and security, in order to reveal the root issue of where our fears stem from. We can then maximize our true identities and lean into our unique gifts due to a grounded belief in our acceptance of others, our acceptance by God, and ultimately, the acceptance of ourselves.

1. AUTHORITY

When we make decisions based on fear, we have given the authority of our lives over to fear itself. When we make decisions based on being accepted by others, we hand the authority of our lives over to them. Until we can answer this age-old-yet-incredibly-relevant conundrum, we are unable to be truly confident in who we are as individuals. Because we all know decisions become very difficult when our authority is found in the flippant opinion of others.

So, who or what do we allow to be our authority when it comes to our own lives? I'm not talking about whether or not you need to be paying attention to traffic lights or police officers. I am talking about the outside voices we listen to—why did you or why didn't you decide to wear your pink wedding dress? Was it because you decided that you actually loved the traditional idea or was it because you saw one too many questioning eyes and confused looks and awkward responses? Only you can answer *why* you make the decisions you make. Why you parent the way you parent. Why you decided to go to law school instead of taking over the family business. Why you decided to be a stay-at-home mom instead of taking that next promotion. That is a question between you and God, and when God becomes the authority in your life, you will be freed to be confident in your decisions instead of being the indecisive eggshell walker you've always been—and that goes for me too. I've been the indecisive eggshell walker. We're in this together.

2. IDENTITY

After you strip away the confusing opinions and preferences that every man, woman, and child on earth will have about the way you live your life, you will be left with a lot less noise and a lot more open space in your heart. When you push the mute button on who and what everyone else thinks you need to be, it can kind of feel like you're on top of a hill, all alone, just you and God. However, this also means pushing mute on that devilish little person inside you who is telling you who you are not measuring up to be. When you push mute on the outside and on the devilish inside voices, it will free up space and time and energy in your heart to sit and be still for a minute with God. Who am I? What do I identify with?

Spoiler alert: Your identity will not be found in your image. It will never be found in your ability to fulfill a certain role. Your identity will not be found in your success. Your identity will also never be found in your own ability to be good enough for God. Your identity is in God Himself. You are made in the image of God, with a purpose that He has designed for you—one of love, authority, freedom, security, and confidence in His approval of you, even when you don't have it from the world.

3. SECURITY

When you understand that you've got God in your corner—made by Him and for Him—you can be secure to be exactly who you are. You can be confident enough that when someone rolls their eyes at that pink wedding gown, you have the courage to respond to them with grace. You can give them a "Heck yes, I did," instead of cowering and changing who you are in order to try and appease someone else. When you feel secure in who you are and in God's love for you and you have been created uniquely to display a part of who He is, then you care a whole lot less about what doesn't matter. And in turn, you can care a whole lot *more* about what actually *does* matter to you.

* * *

Once we are able to name and believe who we are and where our authority is found, we begin to live lives of security and confidence. We begin to own our lives and stop apologizing for them. We cultivate environments of freedom and security for our families and relationships. We cultivate an environment of tenderness with ourselves and truly allow ourselves to begin to be creative and self-expressive.

This self-expression—stemming from having security and confidence—results in the belief that we are worthy of the time we put forth into self-discovery, the time we put forth into our craft and work, and the belief in the love of God. Not because of our own morality and achievements, but because of His achievement on our behalf. When we are secure, we believe that we are worthwhile and can, indeed, pull it off.

And let's be honest, a happy day in Montana with a pink wedding dress, carrot cake, a dance party, and champagne sounds fun. Care to join?

PART

AUTHORITY

ONE

1

THE HEART AUTHORITY

STRINGS OF PEARLS

I remember those long drives down Highway 1.

There was a slight breeze from the cracked window on this midsummer Sunday afternoon. My hands gripped tight on the oversized steering wheel of my father's cherry-red 1969 Chevy truck. The black leather bucket seat sat up high and would bounce slightly as we drove over the small potholes in the road.

Tap, tap, tap, tap, tap, tap, tap, tap.

The sound of my dad's fingers on his laptop as he manually programmed the engine of his truck. My dad is a genius and I always grew up knowing so. This '69 Chevy had the gas mileage of a modern-day hybrid because my dad programmed it that way—adjusting horsepower and torque to maximize fuel economy in the engine by manually programming the laptop he had hooked to the truck's inner workings while I drove. Ya know, simple stuff.

These are some of my most-loved memories with my dad. Those drives were filled with mostly silence and the *tap, tap, tap* of the laptop, but every now and then, my dad would hand me a string of pearls—a figurative string of invaluable pearls of wisdom.

"Hey, sugar, don't do anything to please other people, but do only what God wants of you. Protect your heart."

"Okay, Dad," I would reply as I waited for the rest of what he had to say.

"I will always be here, not to tell you what to do, but to support and help you."

"Thanks," I would say politely, my sixteen-year-old self wondering what all this implied.

"You can be whoever it is God wants you to be, because God loves you. God is not impotent; God is not out of control. He is present and all knowing. So, don't ever let fear stop you. The work of our human nature is fear, but the work of God is courage. When you're filled with joy and hope and peace, you can be courageous. If there's no peace, you can't be courageous. If there's no hope, we won't be courageous. But there is joy and hope and peace—because that is God."

Pearls.

And I wore that string of pearls wherever I went. That's not to say I was always courageous. And it's *definitely* not to say that I never did things just to please other people. But I never believed fear was something to avoid. I grew up believing that there would always be fear along the way and that fear was intended to be a motivator and could always be overcome with courage.

Years later, I was newly engaged to my fiancé and on tour with a rock artist when I received a call from my soon-to-be husband. He had just found out he had been drafted into the Minor Leagues by the Houston Astros. I'll never forget that call: *"If we're going to do this, Jules, this has to be a 'we' thing and not just a 'me' thing."*

I know that we didn't understand completely the implications of baseball life and how much it would change. But we did know that the travel would be intense and that this was going to be a huge difference from what we had visualized for our lives. We had always assumed Ben would become a youth pastor and I would continue being a writer and musician. For two pastors' kids raised in the rural Midwest, the baseball life was uncharted territory.

As weird as it may sound, signing that first professional baseball contract was an act of courage. We had visualized a simple life but signed up for exhilarating chaos instead. I never thought my life would include living between three homes, weekly plane rides, and teaching my children their numbers using hotel elevator buttons. We were fearful of the extremely high divorce rate within professional sports. We were fearful of being apart regularly. We were fearful of being away from family and friends and the very real possibility of isolation. We were fearful of never knowing where we would live, and we knew that a team could trade us and move us without warning.

What is it about fear that can keep us all from living full and courageous lives? Maybe we've lived in fear of putting ourselves out there. Maybe we've lived to just fit in, so that we won't ever have to stand out. Maybe we've allowed fear to keep us from trying new things because, well, if you never try, you'll never fail. Maybe we let fear keep us from being who we are, and we live a life of constant adaptation and pretty pretend.

Most important, what keeps us from fastening that string of pearls around our necks and stepping out in courage, confidence, and brilliance?

TOY BEARS AND CORN SNAKES

The Ancient Greeks and Romans believed courage to be the essential quality in a person. Aristotle wrote, "Courage is the first of human virtues because it makes all others possible."[1] The Roman philosopher Seneca considered all humans slaves to fear.[2] Yet given the right circumstances, ordinary people can set themselves free of this bondage and act courageously. How is this achieved? And what is it that happens to allow a person to willingly choose to engage in an activity that frightens them?

Well, turns out that neuroscientists recently determined how courage works in the brain. There is a little region in the brain called the subgenual anterior cingulate cortex (sgACC), the driving force behind courageous acts. *How did they arrive at this exciting discovery,* you ask?

Teddy bears and corn snakes.

Volunteers were divided into those who had a fear of snakes and those who did not, before undergoing tests with either a stuffed teddy bear or a live corn snake, a nonvenomous species often kept as a pet.

Participants could choose whether to have the toy bear or snake moved closer or farther away from them while a functional magnetic resonance imaging (fMRI) scan was done on their brain.

The scans showed different patterns of brain activity when volunteers succumbed to fear versus when they showed courage by deliberately overcoming it.

Activity in the sgACC increased along with the degree of fear felt by those who had the corn snake brought closer to them despite their fear of snakes. But this was *not* the case with the folks who succumbed to fear by increasing their distance from the snake.

In addition, activity in a series of temporal lobe brain structures was reduced when fear increased but was overcome.

Lead researcher Dr. Yadin Dudai, from the Weizmann Institute of Science in Rehovot, Israel, said: "Our findings delineate the importance of maintaining high sgACC activity in successful efforts to overcome ongoing fear and point to the possibility of manipulating sgACC activity in therapeutic intervention in disorders involving a failure to overcome fear."[3]

And what does this scientific mumbo jumbo mean exactly?

That we have to exercise this part of the brain in order

to overcome our fears. It means that fear will always be present, but there is a definite importance in keeping that little part of the brain active in order to not be *bound to* our fears. That we have to push ourselves to overcome the things we are afraid of.

If you never even *try* to leap over the hurdle between you and living a beautiful, courageous, and brilliant life, you might not ever be able to jump over it at all. That high you get as you are in mid-leap, even if it's just barely grazing the hurdle, is scary—your fear of tripping and falling on your face is legitimate, but it is thrilling. On the other side of that hurdle is courage and confidence and a feeling of complete worthiness. It's a feeling of autonomy that no one but you can give yourself.

I think we can all agree that there is nothing more terrifying than being totally and unapologetically honest— be it when telling the truth or authentically living the life we were made to live. Both Ben and I (here comes the honest part) entered the traveling baseball player/ traveling musician lifestyle with a degree of ignorance. We knew the figures, we thought we understood the risks, but we were unprepared. Kind of like running to jump a hurdle that you *know* is thirty-three inches instead of the normal thirty that you trained with, but you try to make the leap even though you don't know how you will do. Well, Ben and I jumped that thirty-three-inch hurdle and we fell flat on our figurative arses. The travel was a difficult adjustment and the harsh actuality of dealing with public scrutiny was more painful than we wanted to admit. I was traveling every week back and forth between Phoenix and Nashville to try to finish my senior year of college and found myself in the ER with heart arrhythmia due to stress. We were making $200 every two weeks in Minor League Baseball, which was financially strenuous, to say the least. We were in our first couple years of marriage, which is supposed to be so happy and romantic and sexy, right?! But our marriage was on the rocks, and we were both beat down by the difficulty of our uncharted venture. So, we did what so many do when faced with failure and struggle and the fear of others finding out our pain...

We hid.

We hid from honesty. We hid from vulnerability. We hid from any open and honest conversation with family and friends. We thought we were being courageous by staying in the baseball lifestyle—and that *was* the reality when Ben first signed on that dotted line—but when the struggle, isolation, and fear of not being strong enough to endure all the pressure set in, we realized that what was motivating us was no longer courage but fear. We had let fear become the authority of our hearts. Because we were afraid of failing. We were afraid of being looked at as quitters should we not be able to handle it all. We were afraid of what our families would think—that we would be seen as "weak" or "ungrateful for the opportunity" if we were honest about how it was actually really hard. We were afraid that even God Himself would look down on us in disappointment that we couldn't handle the blessings

He'd given us. Our fear kept us bound to performance and bound to striving to keep up a perfect appearance. Our fear of others knowing that we weren't flying high but were actually sinking kept us obsessed with keeping up appearances.

This fear of others' disapproval of us and fear of God's disapproval of us had to come face-to-face with the one thing that would begin to set us free: courage. This time, the courage to be honest and vulnerable. It took the most courage to admit our weakness and come to grips with our humanity and limitations.

Slowly, we began to inch closer and closer to that corn snake of honesty, and when we began to be vulnerable, we began to heal. As our courage grew, it became easier and easier to be honest and vulnerable with ourselves, with God, and with others. We became less and less afraid of being known, and slowly became more and more confident.

Courage is recognizing our weaknesses and simultaneously recognizing that God approves of us amidst these weaknesses. Even though the circumstances didn't change—the travel schedule was still intense, public scrutiny was still a reality, and we weren't making any more money—we began to relish our true heart's authority and live more confident lives.

So how can you train your mind to act more courageously and live a life of authenticity in everyday life?

First, you've got to identify the armor you have *against* being courageous and honest with yourself. You've got to ask yourself, *Why am I afraid, and how am I protecting myself from vulnerability?* Are you masking yourself with perfectionism? Pessimism? Have your feelings of being unworthy led you to always project a feeling of composure? Of having it all together? Or do you emit cynicism? Is sarcasm your chosen tone that best masks vulnerability? (Been there, done it all, folks.)

We must first acknowledge that, yes, fear is a part of life, and, yes, failure is going to reveal that we are not perfect and might even reveal that we feel we are not worthy. Then we've got to expose ourselves to what we are afraid of. We inch ever closer to the corn snake and exercise that little part of the brain so it can grow stronger and stronger, and we will eventually leap over those thirty-three-inch hurdles without a second thought.

I'm sure there are a lot of people who (God bless 'em) have thought I have it all together. The good news is that now you have this book, so you can kiss that perception goodbye! I want people to know that I, too, deal with debilitating insecurities that have taken years and years of exercising that darn subgenual anterior cingulate cortex in order to be a girl who is honest with both herself and with God and a woman who is not shocked by her limitations but embraces them. It took many snakes and hurdles to become a wife who is secure in her marriage and a person who feels her best in clothes that have been compared to the colorful garb of Rainbow Brite (rest assured, you'll hear *lots* about those growing pains in the coming chapters).

GRACE UNDER PRESSURE

Speaking of ensembles reminiscent to Rainbow Brite and the Color Kids, I hear one thing a lot (in both complimentary and not-so-complimentary tones): "I could *never* pull *that* off." Sure, sometimes it's backhanded and sometimes it's genuine vibe appreciation. Either way, I always do my best to hold my head high, even if that head is on top of a crazy, wacky outfit. Much like our decision to take on the baseball/musician lifestyle, I wear kooky clothes simply because I want to. The fun I get from getting dressed outweighs the opinions of others and the desire to please other people (it took me a lot of time to realize that too). Because, truthfully, facing your fear is only half the battle. The other half is having to cope with the risk and uncertainty of the reactions before, during, and after you've faced your fear. Welcoming such critiques takes courage. As Ernest Hemingway so beautifully put it, "Courage is grace under pressure."[4] Can't you imagine him saying this after just taking on an onslaught of bulls and bears and tigers, brushing the minor beads of sweat from his brow and taking a sip from his scotch on the rocks? What he means is that in high-pressure situations, a courageous person remains composed instead of reacting carelessly.

So, courage = practice + grace.

Got it. Pulling it off and courageousness can mean retaining a certain amount of grace, or elegance or poise, when things get a little rough. The figurative string of pearls suddenly seems less figurative.

But, since we don't all have the same je ne sais quoi as ol' Ernie, I also interpret this in another sense. The *other* kind of grace that comes before *that* kind of grace.

Courage, for me, means to be honest and be who I am and wear what I want and live the life I want. But it also means realizing my unmerited favor from God during hard times. When I decide to do something *really* important—something where the projected likelihood of failure is really, really high—the thing that allows me to make the leap is the reminder that *grace* is there even when it's under pressure.

Grace gives us the courage to keep on keeping on.

So yeah, courage = practice + GRACE + pressure.

You can overcome fear with an amazing amount of ease if you simply realize that before all else, you are incredibly worthwhile. You are fearfully and wonderfully made. And I get it—not everyone had a father like mine. But every single one of us living on this little blue planet has a Father who is *constantly* giving us strings of pearls to don and wear proudly every day.

Psalm 139:14 (NIV) declares, "I praise you because I am fearfully and wonderfully made; your works are wonderful, I know that full well." Keep in mind that this definition of *fearfully* isn't the first definition you will find in the dictionary, meaning "full of fear." In fact, in Hebrew, the intended meaning of this word is "with great reverence; standing in awe."[5] To be fearfully made was to be made with interest, with respect, with intimate care and forethought. It meant grace and the knowledge that you were made by something grandiose and supreme. That you were fearfully created to live *without* fear.

And how awesome is the next part: "your works are wonderful, I know that full well"? You are God's work. God has created you with meaning and purpose and intentionality.

What does that mean? It means you are not a mistake. God creating you with intentionality means you are not an afterthought. You are not just two cells joining together and accidentally becoming a human. You were dreamed about, foreknown, intentional, revered, intimately known and cared for from the beginning of time. God saw fit to create you, to allow you to come into this world…and His works are wonderful! Do you know that fully?

If God's works are wonderful, and you and I are the most adored and cherished of His works, then do you believe *you* are wonderful?

How astonishing would it be to believe our worthwhileness and allow that belief to make us courageous! If God has given us implicit worth and value, then what do we have to be afraid of? If God is for us, if He is on our side, then why be afraid of those who are seemingly against us?

HEART AUTHORITY

Pearls are made when a small object, such as a grain of sand, is washed into an oyster. As a defense mechanism against this intruder inside its shell, the frustrated little mollusk creates a pearl to seal off the irritation. A substance called nacre, or mother-of-pearl, is deposited on the surface of the object, forming the shiny, iridescent, smooth pearl.

The object itself (a grain of sand) is not necessarily a bad thing, but to the oyster, it is irritating and is treated as such.[6]

Amazingly, this moment of petulance, pressure, and grievance makes one of the most coveted and beautiful things known to man.

Ralph Waldo Emerson wrote, "The whole of nature is a metaphor," and boy, does that feel most true when it comes to pearls. Emerson believed that the purpose of nature was to give us little pieces of imagery to offer insight into the laws of the universe, and therefore to bring us closer to God.[7] I totally agree, and for me, pearls, and their process of being made, are inspiring representatives of courage being made, practiced, and found in our beloved hearts.

On the left side of your chest is a smooth, round, glowing, gleaming, luminous, elegant, rare, brilliant, soft, distinctive, precious beating thing, about the size of your fist.

It keeps your blood flowing and your eyes open and your brain thinking. Sometimes, unexpected intruders try to make their way into your heart, and those intruders can change the way you see the world and think about the world. When something grabs hold of your heart, that is called your *heart authority*.

So often, I find in my own life that fear has become my heart authority. If I'm afraid of something, I don't want to do it—and if I allow fear to determine whether or not I do something, I have handed my heart authority over to fear itself. Suddenly, every word said and action done can feel shameful and stupid.

Remember, not all oysters have pearls. If you let that intruder take over and don't practice the courage needed, that grain of sand won't become the pearl it was intended to be.

But, the good news is, like the nacre that covers the pearl, we all have been equipped with a heart filter that tells us that we are worthwhile. It can protect us from getting hurt by the silly things the world sometimes tells us. That filter is a strong, resilient, iridescent, and glorious protective layer that turns all the ick to a beautiful sheen. Ladies and gents, if you've got a strong enough heart filter, that pearl of yours can be jewelry grade.

Do you have the necessary filter over your heart that allows certain things to come in and keeps certain things out? Is that little pearl of yours being protected? Or is the wrong heart authority taking over? What on earth can motivate you to live a full, courageous, confident, and brilliant life?

Well, I don't believe you are going to find it on earth. What if our heart authority—the motivation behind our vulnerability and courage—is not found on earth but is actually divine?

What happens when our heart authority becomes something more like "You are fearfully and wonderfully made"? What happens when our heart authority is "You have been made in awe, with intentionality, with worthiness"? When the filter over my heart is the truth that God has made me and His "works are wonderful, I know that full well"? When the authority of my heart is no longer fear but "God saw all that He had made and it was very good"?

That *I* am good. That *you* are good. That you and I are imperfect yet perfectly intentioned. That we are worthy, not because of what we've *done* or *proven* to others or even to God, but because God Himself, from the beginning, set His affection upon us and said, *You are worthy because I have decided that you are.* Grace.

Yes. These are the Father's strings of pearls given to you.

When our heart authority becomes *that*, then and only then will we be courageous. Only then will you and I begin to step outside in bravery and confidence like a perfectly rare and harvested pearl. Only then will our lives look like this sort of gorgeous display of messy, imperfect, and blissfully worthy people in all of our reflective shades of white and gray and luminescent color. Only then will the Scriptures that talk about courage actually begin to make sense, because we are actually *feeling* the fear and are finding ourselves in the situations to have to *be courageous.*

Nothing great was ever accomplished without courage, because the easy things don't need it.

As humans, we become more courageous by being in difficult situations—the same way a pearl is made by the grinding of sand, or a diamond is made by intense pressure, or a tree is made strong by growing to withstand the elements. To pull it off will require courage, because, no, it's *not* easy and, no, it's *not* status quo, and anything that's not easy or status quo will elicit a response. So, we're gonna get tough skin, a solid heart filter, and the right amount of nacre.

We are called to live courageously and confidently. Unashamed and fearless and basking in the illuminating grace of our Creator. Only when we are fully convinced of who we were created to be will we ever begin to step out in courage, confidence, and brilliance.

So, I *dare* you.

Something beautiful might happen.

(And remember, corn snakes don't even bite.)

2
DON'T SHOULD ON ME

ELEVATOR WOMAN

I'll never forget. It was 2009, our first All-Star Game, and St. Louis was buzzing. I was swallowed up whole by a crowd of 45,000 screaming, cheering, whooping (and cussing) fans and I felt as if I were the only person actually *sitting* in the stands—almost everyone else was standing and jumping and dancing.

I'll admit that as the wife of one of the players on the field, I was a bit preoccupied. Rather than rocking out to "Take Me Out to the Ballgame," I was rocking my five-month-old little infant to sleep on my legs. A mixture of Coke, Bud Light, and lemonade—speckled with peanut shells and popcorn kernels floating like little boats in a polluted stream—made its way to my particular place in the stands. I worried about getting the diaper bag dirty, imagining the bag (and the precious Pampers inside) getting totally ruined. So, with one hand I kept a baby still and at rest, and with the other I reached to get the diaper bag. Yes, it was a pretty intense moment if everyone knows the unpredictability of a sleeping child, when suddenly I heard a crowd scream the name of *my* husband.

I'd missed a major play.

Men screaming encouragement and, oddly, women screaming brash and sexual innuendos about my Benny that made me slightly uncomfortable. Should I be offended that that's the father of my child they're talking about? A plastic cup whizzed past my head, thrown by some rowdy fan, and I turned around and thought, *Geez, should I even be here? Am I a terrible mother? Because this doesn't look like life the way I thought it should be.*

I had a pretty normal growing-up experience, raised by a stay-at-home mom and a pastor dad. I grew up in the cornfields of Iowa with a schedule and a life that was the best kind of predictable. I was homeschooled and then attended a private Christian school, followed by a public high school. My mom made my lunch every day and put it in a brown paper bag. Every night after I got home from school or voice lessons, there was a home-cooked meal on the table. My dad would pray and we would talk about our day. For a while I thought, *This is what a family* should *be like.* Cute little ranch-style house. Maybe a golden retriever. Nine p.m. bedtime. I *wanted* to give my children the same stable, loving, white-collar upbringing that I'd had.

But here I was in a world with no how-to parenting books or "national average" consensus. Hubby is a baseball player. Wife here is a working mom—juggling a career as an artist, writer, musician, and, oh yeah, caretaker. More often than not, our "house" is room something-something-something at the downtown hotel. No dog. Two a.m. bedtime.

This is why when Zion was born in February 2009, I was feeling slightly unequipped. I remember the day we found out there was a living, breathing human inside of me. The reality of living a baseball life and having a family hit me like a stampede of angry baseball fanatics: *How will this work? How will we do school and naps and bedtime when my bedtime is two a.m. right now?*

Like all first-timers, I had a stack of how-to parenting books on my nightstand. All very well intentioned, I'm sure, but not one that addressed mothering in a baseball-artist-writer-and-traveling-ten-months-out-of-the-year world. It's terrifying that something as simple as peeing on a stick can make you radically aware that you are now responsible for another human's life. It was terrifying to realize that my shows and my music and my pursuits were all going to have to revolve around this little baby boy growing on the inside.

Obviously, when the time came, I was *obsessed* with his 99th percentile tummy and sweet smile. I was *goo-goo* over carrying him and playing with him and being his mommy. But I was also panicking that I wasn't doing it right.

Eventually, there was no saving that diaper bag at the

game. As I stood up to stretch my legs, I bumped some-one's hand that held a drink and watched it spill every-where. All over the bag. All over my Tampa Bay Rays #18 T-shirt. All over (I hate to admit it) my newborn baby. *What is the point? Should I even try? Should I just give up all this craziness and watch Ben from home?*

On game days, the entire Zobrist clan got a few hours together in the morning and an hour after the game. Sure, it was a little late when we would finally lay our little one down for bed, but it was a time of singing songs and say-ing our bedtime prayers. This nighttime ritual was and still is *precious*. So, this night being like every other, I was excited to take the elevator from the concourse to the tun-nel where we would wait for Ben so we could go home as a family.

The elevator doors opened, and a woman in her forties walked in. It was ten past midnight. She, too, was wearing a Rays T-shirt. She bent down close to little Zion's head. "Mommy," she said in baby talk, "put me to bed! Mommy, I sooo sweepy. Don't be so mean, Mommy. Put me to bed pwease! I should be in bed!"

I went home mortified.

I went to bed crying.

"Ben, maybe I should stop going to games. Maybe I should put Zion on a better routine. Maybe I should give him the structure and the consistency that is in this book... See, read this book right here." I leaned over and grabbed the book off my nightstand—something to the effect of *Parenting 101*. "I read in this book about consistency and routine for babies and how imperative it is to them and their growth."

Ben just looked at me patiently. "But that's not *us*, Jules," he said, and smiled.

"Right, I know it isn't right *now*, but maybe I should quit everything I'm doing. Maybe I should quit traveling with you so I can be home and give him a better schedule."

What this woman did (and what I was then doing to myself) is a classic offense.

One that so often goes unnoticed.

One that often goes ignored.

This woman *should* on me.

Society loves to *should*. We like to *should* on other people. We allow other people to *should* on us. How you *should* look. What you *should* not have worn. What you *should* say. How you *should* parent. When you *should* speak up, when you *shouldn't*. What your love relationship *should* look like. The feminine and masculine expectations attached to living are pregnant with *shoulds*.

And this midnight-elevator woman's *should*ing on me was getting the best of me. *Should I this? Should I that? Should I change this so that obnoxious people don't make me feel bad anymore?*

Then I began to *should* on myself.

Should I give it all up to create a schedule that looks "normal"?

But then I began to think about all the things the lady in the elevator didn't know.

She didn't know that the divorce rate in baseball is 84 percent and growing. She didn't know that Zion is put to bed at midnight but he sleeps until noon. She didn't know that he's fine taking a nap on my lap at the game and is actually quite happy and content about it.

As the realization of what the woman on the elevator was implying deepened, so did my understanding of my own life, and my awareness of the *should*.

I also began to notice how I *should* on myself. *I should really be more like her. I should be more consistent at working out. I should take piano lessons again. I should should should should should.* Like a broken record. *Should*ing on myself, *should*ing on other people.

Yep, it was when I was neck-deep in a pile of *should* that I started to see it all for what it is: deeply personal preferences about living, based upon an individual opinion or life experience, being directed toward someone else.

You are unique and individual, with a unique and individual life. Strangers have not earned the right to speak into how you should be living. Allowing someone to speak directly into your life is an intimate right reserved for *very* few. Because, of the estimated 108 billion people to have ever walked on planet Earth, who has lived *your* life? Who has lived *mine*? Who can say they've walked in your shoes or his shoes or her shoes or my shoes completely? *No one*.

I am what I am and it's high time that I own my reality.

And the reality is this: My name is Julianna Zobrist and I am a writer and an artist and a speaker. I am married to a professional baseball player who travels for the majority of the year. We (now) have three children. My kids see certain hotels and yell, "Yeah! We're home!" They go to a private school for four months out of the year and are homeschooled for the remaining eight months out of the year so we can all be together as a family.

It was time for me to stop living for the approval of other people and get the approval I needed to give myself.

OH, KALE NO!

Let's do a little role-play.

Pretend you are out to lunch with a couple of friends. Let's call them Charlotte and Houston. Suddenly, a stranger approaches your table and says to Charlotte, "Hi! I think your daughter goes to school with my son at Yada Whatever Preschool!" Charlotte laughs and raises an eyebrow and says, "None of our children go to a preschool. We, of course, have nannies or keep them at home because that's what every good mother should do." Suddenly, Houston says, "Actually, I drop off my daughter at Yada Whatever Preschool Monday through Friday! Nice to meet you, stranger!" At that time you say, "I actually drop my kid off at a preschool down the street. It's a great way to socialize them!" What Charlotte is now experiencing is something called false consensus effect.

So, what is false consensus effect? Simply put, it's the tendency for individuals to overestimate the level at which other people share beliefs, attitudes, and behaviors.[1] In other words, Charlotte basically had her own bias about a particular *should* and not everyone agreed. At the end of the day, that *should* was more like a *could* (and that is true almost always 100 percent of the time).

This false consensus effect is significant because it increases self-esteem. It is a confidence-booster rooted in normalizing. *I assume everybody else is doing it too, so it must be right.* But much like the consensus, that self-esteem is fake. It is derived from a desire to conform and be liked by others in certain groups, certain cultures, or certain environments.

That little educational lunch would have been more interesting for Charlotte if Houston didn't say anything. What if all three of us had just agreed? *Oh yes, preschools are terrible. How could you do that to your child? All mothers should avoid it at all costs.* Would you have second-guessed your own choice? Would that *should* make you think again? Would you think that poor stranger was just as pitiful a parent as you?

I know that form of thinking definitely crossed my mind a time or two. We've all been out to lunch, and the waiter comes to take everyone's order. *I'll have a water and the watercress kale salad. I'll have a water and a half order of quinoa kale bowl.* When the waiter gets to you, you really want the bacon and bleu cheese mushroom burger, but everyone else got kale, so you get kale too. No one dares get lettuce, because it just isn't the hot new green reserved for the trendiest of foodies.

Many times, these trends begin with new research

(kale is "the queen of greens"), then the first consumer grabs hold of it (Whole Foods begins to carry a variety of kale-based products: kale chips, kale smoothies, kale guacamole...), and it trickles down through the train of consumerism and popular belief (consensus effect), and now you are *literally* being fed the belief that kale is better than anything else and you should eat it all the time. Suddenly, kale is being used as a method of marketing and masking reality. A kale cookie is still a cookie, full of sugar, preservatives, carbs, and other things. The inclusion of kale in the ingredients of chips and snack foods does not void the reality that you are still eating chips. But false consensus effect—or thinking that "everyone is doing it!"—can lead us to believe we should do this or should eat that. At the risk of you thinking I just really hate kale and no one needs to ever eat it, let me point out the obvious. It *is* good for you. It has been proven to be an excellent source of fiber, high in vitamin K and antioxidants. But it's a food trend, and soon we'll find another green veggie that will grace the plate of every hip farm-to-table restaurant in America.

A trend is something that is always evolving. Always changing. Always rooted in what society is telling us is "in." It's the reason we have food, fashion, and home-decorating magazines. It's the reason the Hollywood carpet is red because it's drenched in the blood of the hopeless What-*Not*-To-Wearers. Trends just for the sake of trends are forms of social pressure forcing us into conformity. (P.S.: More power to ya if you like kale and wear the newest thing from New York Fashion Week, but don't think you're less-than if you don't.)

Our brains *love* new trends because they are just that, new and exciting! Any new stimulus we experience is addressed by our brains to assess the benefits it may offer us—beauty, power, acceptance, fame. We love the idea of seamlessly fitting in to a preexisting stamp of approval.

It reminds me of one of the most embarrassing psychological experiments in human history. In 1951, Solomon Asch conducted an experiment to investigate the extent to which social pressure from a majority group could cause a person to conform. There was a room with eight people— seven who knew the aim of the experiment and one who was a poor, unknowing, clueless guy. The experimenter asked each person, one at a time, to choose which of the three lines on the left card matched the length of the line on the right card. The task was repeated several times with different cards. The answer was always *obvious*.

But when the seven guys gave the wrong answer, the clueless participant conformed. Dr. Asch did this again and again and again. Over the twelve trials, about 75 percent of participants conformed at least once. However, in a control group, with no pressure to conform, less than 1 percent of participants gave the wrong answer.

What does this mean and what was his conclusion?

First, when individuals conform to a group's opinion, even when the group is *wrong*, we observe changes in perceptual circuits in the brain, suggesting that groups and trends and *should*ing changes the way we *literally* see the world. (That's why a trend is super cool one minute and the next minute it looks passé.) Second, when an individual stands up against the group, we observe strong activation in the amygdala, a part of the brain closely associated with fear. Meaning, the reason someone's *should*ing makes us start to *should* on ourselves is because we are *afraid*, so we make decisions, even wrong ones, based on what other people say we should do.[2]

But it is so important to know and be educated on *why* you do what you do. It is important to hold on to your convictions. Being educated about these decisions will protect you from being *should* on by the next health trend or fashion statement and keep you from *should*ing on other people when those *should*s are rooted only in opinion, preference, conformity, a passing fad, or even fear.

The beautiful and glorious silver lining to this experiment that I *love* is that the amygdala response disappears when even a *small* minority speaks up. All it takes is one person saying, "Don't *should* on me!" to lessen this fear response for others.

So, there it is. I'm speaking out against group stupidity and *should*ing. Join me!

DON'T GIVE A *SHOULD*

Amelia Bloomer was about my age, thirty-two years old. A modern girl of the nineteenth century. A part of a fierce girl tribe. She was a writer and a rebel. A fashion icon and a revolutionary. I'm going to flatter myself enough to say that I feel a certain kinship.

She lived in upstate New York, in a sweet little cottage with her husband, Dexter, who ran the local paper, the *Seneca County Courier*. There, she started making a splash as a local socialite—attending every church, community, or political event. Eventually her hubby, Dex, encouraged her to start her own paper, which she did, calling it the *Lily*.

It was that time of year where summer meets dead-on with autumn. The sun feeling a little lazier than it did before, but in that golden sleepiness, it spitefully burns a little hotter. Amelia had been publishing the paper for a few months, talking about women's rights and women's interests, and had decided to take a break from restlessly switching back and forth from writing to editing, to make a quick trip to her friend Elizabeth's house for lunch. Elizabeth Cady Stanton (yes, *the* Elizabeth Cady Stanton—suffragette and all-around girl boss) was a fellow writer for the *Lily* and was having a celebration for her cousin Elizabeth (not too creative with names back then) Miller, who had just gotten back from a trip of globetrotting.

Amelia walked in, donning the traditional long dress that collected dirt and dust bunnies, and saw the cultured and world-traveled Elizabeth Miller in quite the fashion choice—essentially what Amelia was currently wearing as underwear. In other words, straight-up pants. They looked comfortable in this September heat and Amelia was struck with a feeling that all fashion aficionados have: a twinge of jealousy mixed with **Why didn't I think of that first?** But this feeling was less about polish and more about practicality and politics.

A couple days later, Amelia was downtown picking up some flowers for a dinner, when she ran into Elizabeth Stanton. Stanton was walking the streets in a skirt that came a little above the knees and trousers of the same material: black satin. Basically, a skort.

Having been a part in the discussion of the dress question for a few years (refusing to wear corsets or let fashion grip her neck with a choking collar), Amelia decided to practice what she'd been preaching.

A few days later, she donned the pants, and in the next issue of the paper, announced the news. At the outset, Amelia had no desire to fully adopt the style—no thought of setting a fashion trend, no thought that her action would create excitement throughout the entire civilized world.

Days later she sat in her office, amazed at the fury she had unwittingly caused.

Some praised and some blamed and some commented, some ridiculed and some condemned. "Bloomerism" and "Bloomerites" were the headings. Finally, someone wrote "Bloomers," and the name for the garment clung to her ever since.

Hundreds of letters came pouring in from women all over the country making inquiries and asking for patterns—showing how ready and anxious women were

to throw off the burden of long, heavy skirts. The sub-
scription list for the *Lily* ran up amazingly (remember
pre-digital marketing, folks) into the thousands, and
woman's-rights doctrines were scattered from Canada to
Florida and from Maine to California.

Amelia continued to wear the new style on all occasions,
at home and abroad, at church and on the lecture platform,
at fashionable parties and in her office. After eight years, less
and less distaste and dismay and political uproar occurred,
and finally, audiences started to not even notice her clothes
on her body and *did* start to notice her ultimate message—
the question of a woman's right to better education, to a
wider field of employment, and to the voting ballot.

In the minds of some people, the bloomers and
women's rights were inseparably connected. But to this
girl tribe, it was a means to an end.[3]

Point being, those cute Levi's or comfy yoga pants
you're rocking would flat-out not exist if these women
didn't stand up for what pants represented in the bigger
picture. They screamed, "Don't *should* on me if I want
to wear comfy and practical bloomers!" and that fashion
choice in some not-so-small way eventually led to women
having the right to equality.

Sure, these bloomers had many characteristics of a
trend, but the key difference was that these "skorts" represented the power of not allowing people to *should* on
you for the sake of, you know, changing the entire freaking
world.

Because if you want to be a revolutionary in this world,

you must learn to ignore the status quo. To be able to ignore the status quo, you must first be able to see what
"status quo" *is* in our society. Is culture telling you women
shouldn't vote? **Then change it.** Remember, just because
something is the status quo that doesn't make it right.

To use kale as an example again, just because kale is
supposedly a great source of fiber, does that mean you
need more fiber? Is your digestive system depending on
the consumption of *more* fiber? Well, careful, because we
all know what *too* much fiber can do. *Ew*.

Now, let's rewind a couple thousand years and move
nearly 6,000 miles east.

It's another hot day. A guy (also in his thirties) was tired
from his journey, and so he sat down by a well. He was exhausted, weary, his muscles aching and dogs barking, and
he was *thirsty*. This guy was also a kind of feminist and
suffragette in his day, just like Amelia, so when a lady appeared, looking a tad risqué for her day, he wasn't a snoot
or a *should*, but rather asked her for some water.

When he asked her for a drink, she knew what that
meant. In that day, giving and receiving water was an open
conversation (think modern-day, *Can I buy you a drink?*
without the creepiness). He was wanting to chat. He was
hoping to be friends.

"How can a Jewish man like you ask a Samaritan
woman like me for a drink of water?" she asked.

How? Because his name was Jesus, and he was the kind
of revolutionary who wasn't concerned with issues of race
or gender. Gender equality was not even a conversation in

those days; men and women did not converse. Basically, an oil-and-water situation going on here.

But Paul says, "There is neither Jew nor Gentile, neither slave nor free, nor is there male and female, for you are all one in Christ Jesus" (Galatians 3:28 NIV).

All one. Utter equality. Those people freaking out at Amelia Bloomer weren't there yet. We aren't there yet. But Jesus is.

Status quo means nothing because He is and was and always will be way above that. And we can be above that too.

Amelia and Jesus are no doubt friends.

They both had the wisdom and confidence in their own lives to look around, see the status quo, see all the false consensus effects that control conversations, see all the *should*s society and religiosity and culture deem as "right" or "acceptable," and dare to be different. Dare to push the boundary. Dare to press forward, lean in, grit teeth against the opposition, and make a change.

Either way, if anybody tells me that bold fashion cannot point to something more meaningful (i.e., the embodiment of self-expression), I'm gonna give 'em the ol' Bloomer/Jesus spiel.

THEN AGAIN, MAYBE YOU SHOULD

If it isn't obvious already, nothing has exposed insecurity in me quite like having a baby. Having to take maternity leave from music and performing so that my body can heal is always a major test of my pride. And were it not for the loving direction of my husband, I would probably be dancing out on a stage three days later and my uterus would fall out of . . . well, you get it.

I was always afraid my entire career as an independent musician would come to a screeching halt if I took even the briefest of breaks. But in addition to that, there was the obvious glazed-donut-around-my-midsection insecurity. There's just something about my older children asking if I ate too much Jell-O that will always send me into a deep, dark pit of self-doubt even though I had this beautiful, perfect baby in front of me. "But I'm nursing," I would tell myself as I dug into the pack of double-stuffed Oreos.

Ten months after having my third baby, the notorious glazed donut was still sitting around my midsection. I had named it by this point. Mind you, it was more a Krispy Kreme–sized donut now as opposed to a hundred-layer Five Daughters donut (assuming you are missing my reference, you *must* try one if you're ever in Nashville). But still, it was there.

I would say to myself, "Jules, you're ten months post-delivery; you really *should* be able to fit back into your pre-pregnancy jeans."

The *should*.

There it was.

No one was *should*ing on me—most people are decent enough humans to know not to do that after a woman has had a baby, but I was *should*ing on myself. A bad *should*? A *should* that led to more Oreos and self-wallowing? Nah.

I owned that *should*. And I came to the humbling point of realizing that *that should* was a healthy one. I threw the Oreos away. And decided that I probably *should* be drinking more water in a twenty-four-hour period than Coca-Cola. This was a good *should* for me.

Those *should*s can usually be easier to decipher. Most of them can be dealt with a heavy dose of common sense. Your kid is screaming uncontrollably and slept only six hours last night? Probably *should* have naptime. Common sense. I didn't like the extra lingering weight due to overeating Oreos? I scrapped the Oreos. But when *should*s are attached to religion and acceptance or approval by God, they can become very confusing and detrimental to our relational and spiritual well-being.

God-shaming is the term I use any time someone is unable to back up their opinion or preference and resorts to using "God" and "religion" as a way to justify their decision and my need to change.

Think, "Um, Amelia, Elizabeth, and Elizabeth? Those pants are sending you right to hell because they are too sexual and women have no right to bring on *that* kind of attention. It's a sign of moral decline and God would be ashamed."

Or, "Jesus? Talking with that lady at the watercooler is a terrible thing to do, because we all know that talking to women (particularly Samaritan women) is just *not what we do* and I'm guessing you of all people know that God would be ashamed."

God-shame is typically used when someone hasn't

done enough research on their own as to why they do what they do. So instead of having a healthy conversation or debate, they pull out the God Card. Suddenly, God becomes this weapon used to control other people and tell them how they need to be living their lives. Using God-shame is a cheap way to get out of a conversation.

When people use God-shame, it's as if God becomes this big oversized thumb that presses down on you, making no room for inquiry or individuality. A conversation about modesty, for example. Is modesty wearing a floor-length skirt? Is modesty just not showing cleavage? Is modesty not drawing attention to yourself by what you wear? All of these questions are *good* questions. The result of the conversation and dialogue will be different for each individual.

However, to not have a healthy dialogue would be like going over to some of our world's indigenous cultures or developing countries and explaining the concept of "modesty" to them in our Americanized way. The concept must be tailored to them as individuals in their unique situation and reality.

"Well, God says we need to be modest" is not giving any kind of answer. It's a lazy way of ending a conversation using God-shame.

Here's the deal: God does not and never will use shame as a method of motivation.

Guilt? Definitely. Shame? No way.

Guilt is comparing a decision you made to your values and beliefs, then determining that the decision you made was the wrong one. This usually leads to wanting to make a different decision the next time. Shame, on the other hand, is a feeling of humiliation and unworthiness and leads to depression, not better decisions next time. It's the difference between "I shouldn't have stayed with him; he was just manipulating me. That was stupid. I'm not doing that again" and "I shouldn't have stayed with him; he was just manipulating me. I'm so stupid. I'll never get it right." One response recognizes a poor decision as a poor decision, one you don't want to make again. The other response recognizes the poor decision but believes that *you* are the problem who will never be fixed.

Learning to fight "the shoulds" boils down to who and what your heart authority is. Who or what is the heart filter that you've placed over your heart that allows certain things to come in and keep other things out?

Because of our travel schedule and because of speaking and singing in churches all over the country, I am afforded an opportunity to be a part of various churches, how they function, and what they do well. Along with that comes each church's set of "shifting shoulds." Sometimes these *should*s are unspoken, but oftentimes they are spoken and taught loud and clear. They are the opinions and preferences that are not addressed in Scripture that they like to use as a litmus test for spirituality. To speak figuratively, if we are ice cream, then it's not enough to just be ice cream. It doesn't matter that God hasn't asked you to muscle up some whipped topping and Snickers bits, but if you're a *really* good Christian, you have them.

Homeschooling versus public school? Jeans or skirts? Makeup or no makeup? Coffee during church service or no? The church has gone so far as to qualify and quantify our acceptance to God by making the use of an epidural or not a reflection of your Christianity. To write it feels absurd. To read it I'm sure feels absurd. Well, maybe it's because it is just that: absurd.

I believe in a relationship with God that spans cultures and trends and countries and continents and status quo. I believe in the God who looks at me and sees *me*—a human, loving Him and enjoying His love in return. I cannot believe that God is somehow sitting up in heaven giving me more (or less) approval, depending on whether I have a cesarean or a vaginal delivery. And I do not find any evidence of this latter "God" anywhere in the Bible.

You've got to back your *should* up.

If someone is going to tell me how I should or should not live, then they need to be able to thoroughly back it up—and I don't mean back it up with some Google search they did where they found this random blog that has zero scientific or biblical truth. I mean back it up with the Word of God.

If someone is going to be so aggressive as to tell me the way I need to be living my life, then I need to see where God has addressed it in His letter to me. The ability to effectively back your *should* requires knowing and believing who you *are*. The Bible says you *are* loved. You *are* known. You *are* cared for. You *are* special. And holding on to the truth of God's Word can give us such a simple but strong heart filter to live our lives through. We can hold on to who we *are* because He said He accepts us just as such, the way we are. We can be free to grow and change in our opinions and preferences, understanding that growing and changing doesn't change who we *are*. Likewise, other people can have other opinions and preferences because those opinions don't threaten who we *are*.

We have an opportunity to change the culture. An opportunity to stand firm in beliefs that are rooted and grounded in the truth of Scripture and allow all other opinions and preferences to be just that: opinions and preferences. We can be smart, educated individuals who know *why* we believe what we believe, without having to use manipulative God-shame to prove a point. We can be freed to challenge one another, share our research and studies without fear of shame or rejection. We can cultivate environments in our relationships that are empathetic, accepting, and gracious. We can cultivate an environment of honesty and transparency with our children by appropriately addressing their unique viewpoints. We can rest in a spiritual relationship with God that is not sneaky and full of sucker-punching shame jabs, but one of clarity and full acceptance.

The *should*s take their rightful place, and we make sure to always back our *should* up.

OWN IT

The woman on the elevator back in 2009 was uncomfortable with my life.

I don't know why she cared that Zion was up so late. I don't know what chord it struck with her that would inspire her rude comments to me. I will probably never meet her again to be able to ask. But I cannot help but wonder how different my life would be if I had let a stranger's *should* change my life. Oh, if I could go back, I'd be brave and own my life. *Yes, he is still up. And, yes, he is probably getting tired. But my husband, the second baseman in the game you just watched, and I have decided that it is important for him to be on our schedule so that we can be together. So that we can be with him to celebrate his first All-Star Game as a Major League player.*

Once we begin to take responsibility for ourselves and where we are in life, the *should*s hold no more power. And God-shaming can be seen for what it is—a method to control and manipulate, using fear and the name of God to vie for authority over our hearts.

How can you begin to own your life and stop apologizing for it, or casting blame on other people? God has already told you who He is and who you are. We can take the truth of His words and instruction and live freed from all the additional *should*s that people like to throw our way. If we believe what He said is true, then we no longer have to be tossed around by every other person's opinion. When you own your life, you own your happiness.

So what do bedtimes, kale, skorts, and wells have in common?

Nothing really. But they are all opportunities to do what *you* believe is *right*. They are all opportunities to have an awareness of things that don't really matter (parenting 101, kale, skorts, and wells) and of things that so very much do matter (family, health, human rights, and community). So, own your kale *or* not kale. Own your maxi dresses *or* skorts. But whatever you do, do not give any human being the power over you about how you should be living and strip you of your happiness.

EMOTIONAL 3 LAZINESS

ITCHY SHIRTS AND SHRINKING SHOES

There was a period in my mothering experience when I got this anxious, don't-wanna-do-it-yeah-I'd-rather-avoid-it type of feeling every time I had to get my kids in the car to go to the airport. You might be thinking, *Well obviously, airports are like the DMV—nobody* wants *to go.* But my disdain for unavoidable travel days was not because of the airport itself, but rather because my darling five-year-old daughter, Kruse, who on normal days was like a trip down a magical rainbow slide of happiness, would suddenly become more like a not-so-happy face-first free fall from the monkey bars onto the concrete.

Suddenly, her shoes would not fit, her clothes would become itchy, and I would become increasingly more irritated.

"Just get in the car! We're going to miss our flight!" I'd yell. Patience-tank totally empty.

I interpreted her shoe episodes as being defiant and disrespectful. I was annoyed at whatever it was she was going through and (swallowing my pride right now) I didn't want to take the time to help her figure it out. I just wanted her to get it together and get in the freaking car.

It took me a few months to realize the pattern: This behavior only reared its head on our way to the airport.

One day I decided to fix the problem with the biggest paper calendar in the world. I plastered it on our pantry wall and used colored markers to draw when we would be going where and when we would be back to which house. The next time we had fifteen minutes to get out the door and make our way to the airport, the expected happened and she began to cry about her shoes...but *this* time, instead of ignoring whatever it was she was feeling (and thus not helping her define or grow from it, keeping her in an emotionally lazy state), I got down on the floor next to her and held her little face in my hands.

"Girlfriend, what's wrong? I know it's not your shoes; you just wore them earlier today without them hurting."

"Mom, I just don't know!"

"Can I show you something?" I asked her, and stood up to lead her into the kitchen. There on the wall was the oversized calendar with brightly colored markers and poorly drawn airplanes.

"So, we are right here on this day," I said, pointing to the square with the little blue airplane in it. "And right here says 'Boston,'" I continued. "See the line after the airplane? We are going to Boston for these one, two, three days, and then we are flying right back here to Chicago. Right back to this house, where all of your toys and friends and your own bed will be. Did you know that?"

She shook her head.

"Do you want to go see Daddy in Boston and then come right back here to this house?"

She nodded.

"Awesome! Me too. So let's go to the airport now, okay? And we will be right back here in a few days!"

"Okay!" she said, her shoes magically no longer bothering her.

Honestly, I am crying as I think about this because it is heartbreaking that I could have so easily missed this moment. In my flurry and rush and agenda, I could have so easily communicated (by *not* actually communicating with her), "No one wants to deal with whatever you have going on, so just stuff it down. Stuff it down, avoid the emotion, smile, put your shoes on, and deal with it."

My reason for the unkind response was this: stress. It wasn't about the shoes, or the car, or the time. The reaction to the trigger was inappropriate and misdirected. This is emotional laziness—the inability to decipher emotions.

Emotional laziness is a default button we push to avoid discomfort. For me to value comfort (I don't want to really know what's going on and I really just want to make it to the airport on time) over digging in deep with my daughter (asking her what is wrong, opening up that conversation/

can of worms) would mean avoiding the opportunity for vulnerability, trust, communication, and, ultimately, growth. That is grade-A laziness, and if we never deal with the fear or the pain, we get the benefit of ignorance and the result of emotional immaturity.

In the mystery of the shrinking shoes, we were both emotionally lazy. I was the biggest culprit since it's my job to actually teach her about emotional maturity and because I was just getting upset rather than talking with her to get to the root issue. She was emotionally lazy because, well, she was five years old and had every right to be.

WEEPING AT OATMEAL AND PUPPIES

Ladies, we all know how it is when your wonderful "visitor" comes to town each month. A day in the life is painted with an extreme sense of irritability, anger-fused conversations with friends and family, self-pity, low self-esteem, uncontrollable cravings, and just plain meanness. Twelve times out of the year, planet Earth is just not a great place to be.

More often than not, we don't know what it is that we are feeling because we don't know *what* we feel and we have no way of knowing *why* we are feeling a particular way. When we haven't tried to figure out *why* we are feeling the way we are feeling, then we do not know *how* to appropriately deal with or respond to (cue inappropriate emotional reaction), much less grow from, our emotions.

But whether we like to admit it or not (and husbands, you *best* not bring this up in an argument), most of the time we can chalk up this roller-coaster roundabout of emotions to biology. You aren't really crying because the grocery store is out of your favorite oatmeal.

The process of eliminating emotional laziness is blissfully easy: **What** do I really feel? *Imbalanced.* **Why** do I feel it? *Mother Nature.* **How** do I get over it? *Chocolate.*

There is an important lesson to be learned here. Emotions are not the condition. They are merely the symptom. In other words, emotions aren't imperatives; they're not your boss. They're indicatives; they're reports.

It's never really about the oatmeal or the too-tight shoes or getting to the airport on time. It's about imbalanced hormones, anxiety, and time management.

We must learn to allow emotions to play the role they were meant to play as symptoms. The condition is that your friend lost her mother to cancer. The symptom is sadness and empathy and compassion. The condition is that you are discontented in your job. The symptom is complaining about it and, possibly, bitterness.

The condition is that you didn't know the shirt you are buying is 40 percent off. The symptom is happiness and smiles and random hugs to strangers.

The first one is appropriate. The second is likely a need to take control of the situation. The last one is just a plain win.

But there is another beautiful (though sometimes messy) thing about us women. We are *particularly* emotional beings. God gave us an innate ability to empathize and extend compassion.

My mother-in-law is the kind who cries during TV commercials that ask for donations for rescued pets. She experiences this emotional response of compassion because she *feels* for those puppies. She has compassion for the circumstance; she responds with wanting to adopt them all.

I respond differently. Those commercials make me *pissed*. My emotional response is justice. **Who has neglected them? Tell me where those people are and I will make them pay!** My mother-in-law responds with an emotion that I believe is a reflection of God's character. His love for His creation, and His heart for all to have adequate food and water to survive. This is a righteous compassion that can motivate meeting physical needs.

However, I believe my emotional response of anger is also a reflection of God's character. The way that He will make all things right in His time. Call it karma, call it consequence, call it social justice, God will bring every person into account for what they have done. This is a righteous anger that can motivate change.

So, whether people have classified you as an "emotional" person or not, whether you cry at the TV commercial about puppies or you don't, neither response is right or wrong. The way you respond in emotion reflects who you are, and ultimately, God's character!

While emotions can be powerful indicators of beliefs and can provide motivation behind movement, being emotional also means that our emotions can take over and become our sole authority if we do not learn to read and respond to them properly. Especially the dark and painful ones. They can consume our energy, direct our decisions, and rob us of our joy.

Emotions that feel all-consuming are those that are un-dealt with. Remember, in and of themselves, emotions are not the problem (barring mental disabilities or disorders, in which case consult a licensed doctor). To continue to only address a symptom is to completely ignore the real problem. Emotions will reveal something about what you believe, and you must take the time to think through what they are trying to tell you. Because in the end, it's not about shoving down our emotions; it is about how we interpret them and deal with them. And when mis-interpreted or simply ignored, emotions can land us in misdirected sinkholes.

WHAT, WHY, HOW

Betsy and Betty are best friends. They do everything together—they even work at the same place—but they are very, very different. Betsy is constantly strung out; the smallest blip in her day will send her into a state of frus-tration and stress. She is affected by everything around her: the traffic, long lines, a mean coworker. Her mood and emotions are directly influenced by what is happen-ing around her.

Betty, on the other hand, doesn't let stuff get to her.

She decides how she wants to feel and she is much happier in the long run.

So, what's the difference?

Like all forms of laziness, the key factor is choice. In this case, it's a decision to allow your emotions to reveal to you why you are feeling a certain way so that you know you're headed in the right direction or so that you can make a change. Versus the other choice to never appropriately read your emotions, keeping you stuck in a blinded and spinning misfire state.

Are long lines annoying? Always. Can traffic cause you to feel a little anxiety? If you say yes, then congratulations, you're normal! But the most likely difference between Betsy and Betty is that Betsy, without knowing it, has asked the "What?" but not the "Why?"

What's annoying me? TRAFFIC. No thanks. Annoyance. Birds are flipped. Words are said.

But Betsy hasn't asked "Why?" *Why am I so thrown by traffic? Yes, it's annoying, but is traffic enough to throw off my day?*

My guess is, if Betsy had asked herself "Why?" she could probably have landed on a different and *accurate* answer to the frustration behind rows and rows of cars. Perhaps she is allowing her anger to keep her in an emotional sinkhole. Perhaps she needs to broaden her perspective: Traffic in Nashville is nothing like traffic in LA. Maybe she needs to make the best out of the situation: The magical world of podcasts can make for some pretty entertaining and informative car time.

Furthermore, perhaps the real frustration is with herself…how she keeps telling herself to leave twenty minutes earlier to avoid being late but just hasn't made the commitment to getting up at 5:30 rather than 6:00 a.m. And rather than taking responsibility for hitting the snooze button three times, it's easier to shift blame. *It's traffic's fault.*

My guess is that happy-go-lucky Betty is in a practice of taking ownership. She was probably raised with the mantra, "If you can change something, then change it. If you can't, then happiness is a choice." Taking ownership and responsibility for things that are in your control is the "how" part of fighting against emotional laziness.

God gave you the tools to be an emotionally strong individual. He gave you the emotions to point to what you are feeling; then He gave you a conscience to determine why you are feeling that way and the brain power to determine how to respond and take ownership.

SOBER UP, LADIES

When I think about the opposite of sober, I think of somebody drunk at a baseball game stumbling through the concourse, yelling profanities and throwing peanut shells at the umpire. I think of out of control. I think of no physical, emotional, or verbal self-control.

Maybe you haven't ever been drunk from alcohol, but I know for sure I have been an emotional drunkard before.

Saying things I don't mean, misdirecting my emotions toward the wrong person, or overreacting to a false situation I have created in my head. An emotionally lazy person is basically someone who is figuratively drunk in their mind...unable to walk themselves through their emotions without stumbling.

The New Testament contains some verses that use the term *sober-minded*. This is always attached to a command to *be* sober-minded. I get what it means to *be* sober. If you ask anyone, "Hey, are you sober?" there's no confusion as to what you are asking. But sober-*minded*, now, that's not one we use very often with one another. Being *sober*-minded is to not be drunk in your mind. To be clear-headed, able to walk the line of truth and error, and bring clarity and truth to the road map of emotions.

When you are sober-minded, you look at life through a lens of truth.

Consider this situation: You're crying and upset that your man didn't *love* the half-baked, salmonella-ridden chicken parm that you made for dinner. Suddenly your emotions have taken you down a road of self-pity and untruth: *I'm the worst cook ever. He will never like anything I make ever again.*

Now he feels bad for just saying, "Hey, babe, I think this is undercooked," and probably would have said nothing except that, in this case, he'd get food poisoning.

That's driving emotionally drunk (and at the risk of harming other people). So, let's sober up and look at life through the eyes of what is actually true:

1. You're not the *worst* cook ever. There is no doubt that I am worse at it than you.
2. He's a guy; he's going to want to eat.
3. That chicken parmesan *was* bad because it was undercooked.
4. Own it.
5. You're crying because you're embarrassed. Don't worry—we all get embarrassed sometimes.
6. Throw in a frozen pizza and learn the art of laughing at yourself!

If emotions are like the needle on the compass of your heart, sober-mindedness is the ability to read the compass and know which direction you are headed. Sober-mindedness is the "what and why" report manager that will give a clear read on where you are and what you are headed toward. Only when we have the ability to read this compass accurately will we be able to answer the "how?" *How does my course need to change? How can I get to where I want to go? How can I fix the fact that I'm off the path I want to be on?*

This compass will always tell the truth. No beating around the bush. Only the straightforward, simplistic truth of where our hearts are. This compass also does not lie. If you're headed southwest, it's not going to point due north. If you are spinning in circles, then that needle of emotion will be spinning along with you.

I don't believe that God discriminates among directions. South, west, north, east, He made them all—anger, compassion, justice, sympathy, sorrow. He has felt them all and they all deserve to be listened to. We don't pit reason against emotion, because in order to use a compass, you need a needle and a map to go along with it.

.

THE EMOTIONAL ROAD MAP

Here's some good news for you. You were not left simply with a needle that changes direction as your emotions change. You were not just given a compass that shows you which way you are headed. You were also given a map that shows you what you are headed toward and a brilliant conscience to guide your actions.

The Psalms of lament are a rich resource for learning about *how* God desires us to express, address, grow, and learn from our emotions. The laments are those psalms in which the psalmist expresses the deep pains and heartaches of life. They are the psalms where the writer cries out to God about hard emotions such as sorrow, fear, grief, and abandonment. In reading the Psalms of lament, we can learn how to face our own emotions.

And despite there being basic emotions and complex emotions, this little guidebook is sure to cover all the bases.

You can pull an easy twenty-four: loneliness, love, awe, sorrow, regret, contrition, discouragement, shame, exultation, marveling, delight, joy, gladness, fear, anger, peace, grief, desire, hope, heartbreak, gratitude, zeal, pain, and confidence.[1] God gets angry. He gets lonely. He loves. He has loyalties. He gets jealous. He feels compassion. Jesus felt afraid. He weeps.

The emotional needle of life will probably point to every single emotion over the course of a lifetime. Learning how to express and address where we are and grow and learn from these emotions—putting one foot in front of the other on the path we feel called to be on—is the goal.

You've got to look at the compass, and you've got to read it correctly—and if you're mentally drunk, you won't be able to read it clearly, and your emotions will run wild and take over the entirety of your heart authority. So, sober up, ladies! Let's stop spinning in circles. Let's stop and take a long, hard look at our emotional compass. What is my emotion pointing toward? What is really happening here? I'm not drunk in my mind; I can read this clearly. Or maybe my mind is a little drunk right now and I need to hydrate and maybe take some aspirin and *wait* until I can have a meaningful conversation with my daughter when she thinks her shoes are too small. Where does the needle say I am pointing? And now, what is my self-controlled response to my next step?

Emotional maturity takes courage, and as we know, it'll take practice and grace under pressure. Emotion and pain and struggle and rough climbs up tall mountains and drives into the deep valleys are unavoidable, but the road map is not for your ease; it's for your good! I believe my ability to read the map of life is God living with me, beside me, in me. My Holy Spirit, my conscience. God promises that if we rely on the Holy Spirit, He will help us. Galatians 5:22–23 (ESV) says, "But the fruit of the Spirit is love, joy, peace, patience, kindness, goodness, faithfulness, gentleness, self-control; against such things there is no law."

When we are faced with a confusing compass reading, or we discover that we are feeling an emotion that is pointing us down a path we do not want to go, we have not been left alone. We have not been told there is no way around what is in front of or behind us. When we stop to observe the map and the landmarks that God has placed, and we listen to His Spirit, we can respond to the needle readings with joy and peace and self-control!

So, the next time your shoes feel too tight or your shirt begins to itch and you want to yell at the first person who doesn't want to eat your undercooked chicken, take a good look at your compass.

VERBAL GYMNASTICS

GOING FOR THE GOLD

Nothing is more deeply disturbing than a conversation gone awry. Suddenly you feel yourself walking the tightrope of understanding, jumping through hoops of passive-aggressiveness—a couple of emotional backflips later, you land clumsily on the vault of big little lies. Ladies and gentlemen, you've just found yourself competing in verbal gymnastics. And guess what? Everybody loses.

But one fateful summer afternoon, I was going for the gold.

The unpleasant ringing of my 5:30 alarm woke me up in yet another hotel in yet another city. I nearly fell out of bed trying to turn it off as quickly as possible in order to avoid waking my sleeping husband and three kids.

I tiptoed to the bathroom, where I had all my clothes and shoes and makeup set out from the night before (forward thinking for the win). I did my best to look sharp and then hopped in the car to make my way to two back-to-back interviews at the local TV stations before returning to the hotel, where I would find my sweet little family in the restaurant having breakfast before heading to the pool.

So I did the quick switch out of my full-flowered body-suit and culottes into a color-blocked swimsuit and towel and rushed down to the pool, donning the figurative mommy hat along the way.

The day was shaping up nicely by all accounts—we drowned ourselves in sunscreen, played in the pool, had a nice lunch outside, played in the pool some more, and then, always working at least ten steps ahead of myself, decided we needed to go in for naps.

The kids can sleep from 2:00 to 4:00 p.m.; that will give me two hours to finish up some work, and then I can help them with homeschool until 5:00, order dinner at 5:30; it will arrive to the room by 6:00; we can eat until 6:30, and be on time for the game. Phew. Perfect.

The Zobrist clan, dripping wet and wrapped in hotel towels, made their way to the room to execute this perfect routine. One kid was whining for a snack and the other was just whining and saying, "Nap, Mommy, nap?" *Yes, girlfriend. You're going to take a nap.* Zion rushed to push the button for the fourth floor and that *ding!* could not have come any faster.

I was feeling the weight of being exhausted and the evening schedule ominously looming in the distance, not to mention the guests we had to entertain at the game tonight, and oh yeah, that deadline I was supposed to make last night that didn't happen so I had to make it happen today.

Ding!

As we were walking into the elevator, arms full of a baby and towels and sunscreen, I asked my husband, "Do you have a key, babe?"

"No, I assumed you had one."

"How could you have assumed I had one when you left for the pool without me? You left the room when I was still on my way back, so I can't imagine how whether or not *I* had a key was a reason for you not bringing a key to the pool."

Not much to say after that.

In silence, we pushed the lobby button again, hopped back off the elevator, went to the front desk, got a key, and walked back to the elevator.

Fourth floor, room 410. Finally. Run.

The kids were tucked in for their naps by 2:00 p.m. The routine went executed as planned, with only a minor stumble: 7.0.

Success! Now I get to shower and finish the writing I've got to get done before they wake up. The clock was ticking.

"Hey, Juuuules," my husband said in a way that was easy to read. He was wanting some "special" mommy and daddy time.

I was tired from being up at 5:30 a.m. and had already penciled in doing some work from 2:00 to 4:00 in my mental daily planner. Plus, the whole *I assumed you would have a key* comment just left me annoyed and frustrated.

In other words: not in the mood.

But I tried to make some sort of dishonest, slightly passive-aggressive, clearly-not-saying-what-it-is-I-was-needing-to-say cartwheel, and dang it, he just knows me too well. I fell flat on my face.

Fast-forward through the thirty-minute episode of the ultimate Olympic Games of Verbal Gymnastics.

The "no, nothing's wrong, you're just reading into things" big little lies. The "I'm fine, I can handle it" but really what that means is "I don't want you to see my weaknesses" backflip. The "I'm so sorry for you that you woke up basically when I had already done *two* shows" passive-aggressiveness. The "How could you forget a key? Did you forget sunscreen for the kids too?" heart-authority takeover.

Verbal gymnastics can last only so long. Every gymnast needs a break and a sip of water from her Nalgene bottle. I broke.

What I should have said?

It's not you. I am just off. I am not okay. I am frustrated with how tired I feel; I am frustrated with work; I am frustrated with business; I am frustrated with my current schedule; I just need more time, more sleep, and less people.

But, alas, instead of simply telling him the truth—that I needed a break, that I maybe needed to nap today, that I maybe needed some help figuring out some logistical things—I took it out on him.

Why is it so hard to just say what we mean? Why is it so much easier to dance around the subject or sweep things under the rug? Why do we perform this verbal gymnastics routine with one another when we could just say what we mean?

Because it's easy. It is so much easier to use metaphorical hyperbole, because the moment you are asked a direct question, you always have a loophole.

"Jules, maybe you need to take a break and rest today?"

"No, I never *said* I was tired. I am fine. I just wish that when you had the kids you would remember to bring the freakin' key with you. Now we've wasted time arguing and I'm behind and I have all this catching up to do. When are you going to get it?"

No one was really sure what I was trying to say; therefore, I was always able to deny any accusation and take control of the conversation again if I needed to. Worst of all, I wanted to hurt Ben in the process. There was a little part of me that wanted him to feel *bad* about what he did.

Not pretty.

A skilled verbal gymnast like myself is strong in her ability to control a conversation. This is the key difference between verbal gymnastics and emotional laziness. Emotional laziness comes before verbal gymnastics. It's not taking the time and energy to figure out the root issue. It's not about control of the other; it's about losing control of the self. It's passivity.

Verbal gymnastics, on the other hand, use *too* much time and energy to take control of the other person's heart authority. It's the symptom of emotional laziness. It's warfare. A verbal gymnast is flexible in her ability to say, "Don't twist my words; that is not what I was saying." To get out of her ownership. A verbal gymnast is the girl who hasn't taken the time to know exactly what she *is* feeling... She just knows she doesn't want to be the one to blame for anything, never wants to be the one to have to own her opinions.

The room key? The key was absolutely *not* the problem. But in an effort to protect myself and not have to actually *confess* that I needed help or that I needed a break, I made it about something as stupid as a little rectangular piece of plastic.

YOUR GUIDEBOOK TO MANIPULATION

"Aaaaaaaand here comes your champion, ladies and gentlemen—bajillion-time gold medalist known for the way she enters the floor unnoticed... No one even saw her and her team enter today. She is a master at masking her presence. We never know how she will be disguised, so we all wait with anticipation, walking on eggshells until she reveals herself. Known for her improvisational routines and her perfected and unexpected backflip technique, it's no wonder the newbie gymnasts are nervous around her! This competitive sport comes down to a competition for control, and, folks, she is the ninja of all ninjas in this verbal gymnastics game!"

To win the gold medal in verbal gymnastics takes precision and practice in various disciplines. It takes a lot of time utilizing the Passive-Aggressive Balance Beam, Belittling Still Rings, Pommel Horse of Ignorance, Sarcasm Vault, Tumbling Condescension, and swinging on the Uneven Bars of Insecurity.

But in an effort to shoot it to you straight, let's just get down to it, shall we? I mean, we've all felt it. We have all been the person just minding their business, having a conversation, and then suddenly the person in front of you does a double backflip, sticks the landing, and you are left asking: *Wait, what? What just happened?*

What is happening when suddenly the tables turn and you get this weird feeling that the conversation you are having with someone is *not* really what is going on. In these moments, you, my friend, have just become the victim/trampoline/audience/observer to someone else's verbal gymnastics routine.

We need to be able to identify *when* this is happening and exactly *what* is happening if we are ever going to know how to combat it. So, let's run down a few of the ways people use verbal gymnastics against us to gain control:

1. **Passive-aggressiveness:** Any type of successful attempt at manipulation or desire for control

of your heart authority can be translated as some form of passive-aggressiveness. It's covert in its nature but intentional in its ferocity. Passive-aggressiveness most often occurs when the aggressor is trying to ignore their own feelings. Rather than being up front and honest about what he or she is feeling, the passive-aggressive person insists, "I'm not mad," even when they are seething on the inside. Passive-aggressive people use words like *fine* or *whatever*. Which when processed through the translator of truth says: "I'm not fine. I *do* have something to say, but I don't want to be honest. I just want this conversation to be over and hurt you in the process."

2. **Ignorance:** *Oh, gosh, I thought you knew!* is the classic tale of a verbal gymnast. Avoiding any responsibility is their goal. If they plead ignorance, then they can never be held responsible. This leaves the victim feeling left out and helpless, while the verbal gymnast gets a free pass because they "just didn't know!"

3. **Sarcasm:** This is a tricky, tricky backflippy one. While it can so easily be written off as a form of humor, sarcasm can produce many hurtful things all in the name of joking. Sarcasm is even trickier when the verbal gymnast realizes you are *not* laughing at their joke, and now, sensing your hurt, continues in their own self-protection:

"Geez, don't be so sensitive." The verbal gymnast is a mastermind at using sarcasm to be cruel. Sarcasm will ruin relationships by causing bitterness, pain, and insecurity in one individual while the other walks away—the domineering "funny" abuser.

4. **Belittling:** Verbal gymnasts are masters at indirect hostility. They sometimes even use terms of endearment as weapons against the individual they are speaking to: "Hi, sweetie." When the individual gets tired of the belittlement or worn down by the condescension and finally blows up and gets mad, this is when the verbal gymnast performs at their best. The gymnast then acts shocked at the individual they've angered, questioning their self-control and pretending to be hurt at the "overreaction."

5. **Playing on insecurities:** This discipline of the verbal gymnast is particularly frustrating to me. Imagine yourself at the zoo, standing at the fence looking into the den of a majestic and fierce lion. You are reading the description to your little girl when suddenly you hear a woman's voice next to you. "Come on, Davie!" she calls out sweetly to her four-year-old son, who is captivated by the dangerous wild animals. She begins to push her stroller carrying Davie's younger baby sister and calls again, "Let's go and see the monkeys!" But Davie is now enraptured

by the squirrel hopping from tree limb to tree limb right into the lion's den. With great concern, he says, "Look, Mommy! That squirrel is going into the lion's den!" The mom, now fifteen feet away, hollers in frustration, "Yeah, and that's going to be you if you don't follow me right now! Come on! Let's go!" Davie, ripped out of his nature fantasy, jumps to his feet and begins to run as quickly as his little four-year-old legs can carry him, fear written all over his little face.

First off, moms, I implore you: Do *not* play on your children's fears. Verbal gymnasts will feed off the insecurities instead of doing the hard work of patiently teaching children how to listen to instruction. However, they will do it to their peers too—"Oh, you're *sure* about that?" It plants the seed so that when the victim second-guesses, the verbal gymnast can manipulate the outcome.

Now that we've identified the everyday ways people vie for our authority, we can stand in a posture of confidence, ready to defend the self-assurance that is rightfully ours. But since you can't fight verbal gymnastics with *more* verbal gymnastics, how do we remove our gymnast uniform and confront and expose the fancy footwork for what it is?

HOW YOU COMBAT VERBAL
GYMNASTICS

All right, so we've aimed the spotlight and turned up the voltage. We're aware and prepared to start identifying verbal gymnastics in others and in ourselves. Let's talk about how we combat the verbal gymnast. How do we approach someone who is not being honest or who is even being secretly hostile in their communication?

1. When you find yourself face-to-face with a gold medalist in passive-aggressiveness and you hear "fine" or "whatever" when she is obviously *not* fine with whatever it is that you're discussing, don't let it slide! Neglecting those things creates bitterness in everybody. The best thing to do here is approach it head-on. "Hey, I can tell you're not fine. Please be honest. What's going on?" A verbal gymnast typically needs time to process their emotions aloud, because typically they are not aware of what set them off into Fine-Whatever Land to begin with.

2. If someone plays the ignorance card and says, "Oh, gosh, I didn't mean *that*!" when clearly they meant *something*, much like how you would deal with passive-aggressiveness, I would confront that head-on too. "Then what *did* you mean? Please explain to me in honest words. You, not I, are responsible for your own words."

A verbal gymnast must see that he or she cannot just assume, suggest, or hint at things and expect everyone to read between the lines.

3. I will never forget when Ben and I started dating. At first our flirting was awkward just like everyone's...slightly planned, kind of contrived, and always awkward. After a week of awkward sarcasm in an effort to flirt, Ben suddenly stopped. "Let's vow, from now on, to always be tender with one another." "What do you mean? We're just joking!" I responded, still laughing. But then he explained himself. "I never want you to be the brunt of my jokes and I don't want to be the brunt of yours. Let's promise to always be tender and to always say what we mean. If we want to joke about something, it is never at the other person's expense." I was moved by his sensitivity toward me, and we shook on it. From that day on, twelve years later, we try our best not to be sarcastic at the other's expense. If it does happen, we remind each other, in love, to always be tender.

Sarcasm is such an easy way to laugh or poke fun without being "serious." But I compare sarcasm to getting a paper cut. Yeah, it might sting for a second, but you probably won't even get a Band-Aid for your paper cut. Not a big deal, right? Well, the next day, if you get another paper cut in the same spot, it's going to hurt a little bit more. Slowly, paper cut by paper cut, something so small can begin to bleed, and if ignored long enough, those hundreds of tiny paper cuts can become a massive cut. And if infection sets in, it can become a massive problem. The next thing you know, you're at the doctor for ignoring the hundreds of little paper cuts.

4. "*Honey*, you're going to have to want it more than that if you want to be successful," the man said to me at a record label meeting. He had just spent the last thirty minutes sharing the plan for a tour and recording my next record, and what it would take for me to truly be successful in his mind. I responded to his daydream, saying, "But the thing is, I'm a mom of three irreplaceable kids and the wife to a man I happen to be obsessed with. I don't want to be gone from them for four months at a time without the option in the budget of them traveling with me." The reality was that the contract wasn't where it needed to be for me to sign with them. So what did he resort to? Not to owning what they would offer. Not to a polite or gracious (even while being disappointed) understanding of my commitment to my family. No, instead he resorted to belittlement out of his insecurity. To which I responded, "Well, I don't want your version of success. So I guess this meeting is over."

When someone belittles you, however big-money or big-business they are, stand up for yourself. You are worth more than the *honey* they are trying trap you with.

5. Playing on insecurities is a tough one. This one takes some guts. This one takes a lot of vulnerability. When someone is using something they *know* you are insecure about as a way to manipulate you, remember that as much as you want to be defensive and pretend the insecurity isn't there, that absolutely will not work. The verbal gymnast *knows* you are insecure in that area, which is why they are using it against you. Instead, being honest about how it makes you feel is the best way to face this. Don't try to be tough. Instead, explain with love and care that it is hurtful for that person to use what they *know* you are struggling with as a method to manipulate you. Call it what it is: manipulative and wrong.

Trust me, I know this can get heavy. Emotions are complicated, and feelings are real. The reality is that I have seen myself play the part of the verbal gymnast in each of these scenarios. None of us is exempt from falling into our insecurity and attempting to control others so that we aren't found out. We've all done it. We've all *felt* it. But when you see it in yourself, the necessary action—by no means easy and probably the hardest thing to do—is very simple. Be vulnerable. Be honest. Apologize. Take the gold medal of verbal gymnastics from around your neck, lay it on the table along with your ego, and be transparent. Say what you mean and mean what you say. Only in this foundation of vulnerability and honesty will you truly be aware of how words are so powerful that they can redefine how you see yourself and those around you. And that same vulnerability and honesty will eventually bring about meaningful and honest communication and community with others.

THE PARABLE OF THE PORCUPINE

Using the art of verbal gymnastics to keep a safe distance feels so much more comfortable than a heart-to-heart about the true needs of the people involved. It reminds me of a parable about porcupines by the German philosopher Arthur Schopenhauer.

It was a cold winter's day and a bunch of cute little porcupines were huddled together for warmth. However, when they huddled together, they began to prick one another with their quills and they were forced to separate. A bit later, they huddled together for warmth again, but their sharp quills pricked and prodded, so they drew apart and became cold again. At last, after multiple rounds of huddling and dispersing, they finally discovered that they would be better off remaining at a safe distance from one another. They had to keep adjusting their closeness and distance, balancing their needs to keep warm with the risk of getting too close.[1]

This safe distance didn't allow them to be as warm as possible, but it kept them from hurting one another. The mutual need for warmth was somewhat satisfied and all the porcupines slept okay... until the next gust of wind blew.

We're not porcupines. So, why do we treat our loved ones like they're covered in prickly needles? We've mastered the art of guardedness for self-protection but at the cost of the vulnerability and closeness necessary for warmth of true intimacy.

This drawing together and backing out is done continually through words—not only in the heart-to-heart talks that occasionally are necessary to untangle the knots we have talked ourselves into (and that often get us even more tangled up), but also in the seemingly meaningless conversations of daily life. *Where's the room key? Where's the sunscreen? Why can't you ever just decide what's for dinner?*

Verbal gymnastics makes every interaction and conversation an activity comparable to picking your way through a minefield. It moves beyond verbal and into the nonverbal cues that make miscommunication so freakin' sticky. But if it happens so often that we have such a hard time figuring out what the other means, why do we keep resorting to it? Why don't we just say what we mean?

If only we could take a good, hard look at ourselves and say, "Whoa! Did you notice that we have these prickly quills that make us this way?" Instead, we both do things and say things to inch further and further away from each other. And in the end, that is *way* more painful than a thousand little stabs from porcupine quills.

We are a world *filled* with verbal gymnasts and lonely

little porcupines. We dance around subjects and never truly say what we mean. We fail to take responsibility for how we really feel and instead take the road of the lazy chick's doctrine. We manipulate the ones we love most and we allow others to manipulate us. We let verbal gymnastics trick us into letting others be our authority. We fail to be intimate and vulnerable with others.

A commitment to being honest is risky business. Sometimes it will feel like there is nothing to catch you. No soft, cushy padding. Sticks are bound to be thrown. Bones are bound to be broken. Clumsy backflips may leave some bruises because, yep, words *do* hurt. Being honest means that there is more to lose. If I'd been honest with Ben about my capacity that day in the hotel room, would that mean I'd have to say no to things in the future? That's a scary type of question to ask yourself.

But this commitment to honesty, vulnerability, intimacy, and transparency is the only way we can have pure relationships with others. It's how we have deep friendships and marriages. It's putting on your big-girl pants and taking responsibility for how you feel and what you do while still knowing that there are always people who are going to use verbal gymnastics against you.

But now you know the backflips and tumbles and spins to see them when they're coming, and you can be guarded against being wounded. The words will hurt a little less, and you'll be more happily concerned with the warmer (though still painful) porcupine quills.

5

EYES WIDE OPEN

THE PITCHER'S MOUND

Sometimes I daydream.

And on a particularly sunny day, I found myself standing in the concourse of center field overlooking the diamond with its perfectly manicured green grass and sterile white bases. I was staring at number 18, who was playing left field that day. I was lost in thought about how we met and how far we've come. (And I may or may not have been staring at his butt in that tight uniform... *I mean, can you blame me?*)

When I think of my husband and me, I think of him as the still waters running deep in the ocean and me as the playful waves that keep the tides moving. He's the unshakeable necessity of black and white and I am every shade of gray and off-white. Ben is the steady rhythm that can sometimes go unnoticed in a song but that gives it its foundation. He is the four on the floor, and I am the off-beat snare and melodic synth. He is the salt of the earth, and I am consistently amazed by his steadfast goodness.

"YOU BETTER GO KILL YOURSELF IF YOU'RE NOT GOING TO MAKE THAT PLAY!"

Cue the screeching tires. Crash landing. Grenade explosion right in the middle of my love-fest daydream that brought me back to reality.

Yikes, what happened? I thought, just in time to catch the tail end of the replay on the big screen. Apparently, the main character (well, only character) in my daydream had missed a play and was now having death wished upon him by a stranger in a jersey with a Bud Light in hand.

I resisted the urge to try my best Wonder Woman skills out on the man, but alas, they won't allow shields into a baseball game. How could someone say something like that to someone they don't know? Would anyone actually say that to someone they *do* know? What is it about sports that make people think that along with their ticket comes the right to act idiotic and say cruel things? What is it that allows anyone to think it's ever appropriate or okay?

I was mad, y'all. And it took me a few innings and a few laps of pacing around the stadium to get my heart rate back down to normal.

It was a strange thing: that within the same singular moment, at the same place in time, the same human could be the object of so much love and so much hate.

And just as quickly as I was brought out of my day-dream I was taken back into another one.

But this dream was different. I sat in this very stadium, filled with the same 50,000 people, but I saw a completely empty field. No one was in a uniform; no one was on first base or behind the plate. One lone usher opened the side gate by the third-base dugout, and the clank of the metal lock dropping could be heard by every observer in attendance. As the usher stepped through the gate and onto the dirt, he motioned to the first individual in the first row to come forward. Slowly and somberly this man sporting a red T-shirt walked to the pitcher's mound. He held his hands to his sides and stood there in silence for only two seconds, but what felt like an eternity to him. Suddenly the stadium erupted in both applause of confirmation and boos of disapproval. He hung his head and slowly walked back off the pitcher's mound, this time to the big gate in right field where the first base line meets the back wall. He walked through the gate, and a sticker with the letter *D* was placed on his chest. ***Disapproved.*** The man in the red T-shirt disappeared into the horizon.

My eyes turned back to the field.

Next, a young girl about four years old skipped to the pitcher's mound. She blissfully sat crisscross applesauce on the mound of dirt, drawing hearts and stars and her name in the red sand. ***Surely, she will be approved,*** I thought. Yet somewhere—way back in the cheap seats of the outfield—a woman began to boo. Others retaliated in applause, and seconds later the stadium was roaring in opposition. The young girl was directed by the usher to the side gate and received her D sticker. *Disapproved*.

The stadium fell silent again as a breathtaking woman glided through the gate and toward the mound. She walked with confidence and stamina and purpose. If there ever was a lioness embodied in female form, it was her. All I could think was that if anyone had a shot at being approved by this entire stadium, it would be someone like her. A virtual goddess. Yet, just as those before her, and just as each and every person who followed, she was met with a blend of approval and disapproval. *Disapproved*.

Fifty thousand people in the stadium. Who among us is 100 percent approved?

Standing on the mound, we all ask the question, "Am I completely approved? Does everyone agree with everything I have ever said, ever done, ever worn? Every person I have ever hung out with, every decision I have made for my family, every career move, every social media post, every food choice?" Who among us can say they are totally approved by the world?

The answer is a sobering one: not a single soul.

You will never meet a person that you agree with 100 percent of the time. At some point, even for someone you know deeply, intimately, you will disapprove of a decision they make. And for me? There is no way that I will ever be able to stand on that mound, met only with applause.

I awoke from my daydream with the roar of the home crowd around me as we ended the inning. The fans in opposing colors sat down. My new understanding of humankind that day was a revelation to me. Without ever verbalizing it, I realized that I had probably thought there was a chance that *if* I tried really hard and *if* I gave sacrificially and *if* I lived with integrity and *if* I lived in love, that maybe, just *maybe* there would be a chance for me to walk onto that mound and be approved by all mankind. But as the man screaming at my husband proved to me that afternoon, that would never be the case. There is not one among us who can be successful enough, kind enough, beautiful enough, or generous enough to ensure approval of all mankind.

You might think this was a depressing revelation for me—you know, a good time to dig a hole and find the nearest bar of chocolate—but that was not the case.

Because this revelation was pure liberation.

SWEET LIBERATION

One of our more lasting social misconceptions is the idea that what others think of us actually matters. While this idea clearly has primal roots, its shift from survival instinct to a social-life essential has become one of our greatest obstacles to self-acceptance and confidence.

Sure, there was a time when our ancestors shared the planet with saber-toothed tigers and wooly mammoths, where the worst thing that could happen would be to get left behind to fend for yourself. Group inclusion was absolutely necessary for survival.

Today, our greatest predatory threat is no longer Jurassic creatures, but our very own friends, neighbors, and loved ones. The need for acceptance—and the fear that we won't be accepted—remains a powerful influence on our thoughts and feelings. In fact, this in large part drives the existential anxiety that has become the trademark of a generation—driving everything from people-pleasing to verbal gymnastics to codependence to oversharing on social media.

Every little action committed, word said, thing thought, outfit worn, emotion felt is up for criticism. The nineteenth-century writer Elbert Hubbard gave a little bit of sage anti-advice: "If you fear to be criticized, say nothing, do nothing, be nothing."[1]

In other words, if you are going to be met with some kind of disapproval or criticism no matter how hard you try, then you have a big decision to make. Either ignore your inherent imperfection, incessantly looking for the approval that you will not find, living bound and shocked any time someone disagrees with you or doesn't like you, or live with the alternative: feeling liberated and confident.

With the latter choice, I can be liberated and comforted by knowing that I will never receive what I think I want (approval of mankind) because in actuality, what I really *want* is approval from God. But here's the key piece of information that changes the game: I already have it. "Be strong and courageous. Do not be afraid or terrified because of them, for the Lord your God goes with you; he will never leave you nor forsake you" (Deuteronomy 31:6 NIV).

The end of the daydream (which, spoiler alert, is reality) comes when you realize that God Himself has approved you. When we look to the righteous perfection of Jesus instead of ourselves, we have *complete* and *full* acceptance from *God Himself*! And, oh man, *that* belief vaporizes the need for constant affirmation from others. And what you find is confidence—confidence in God's promises and approval.

Suddenly the verse "If God is for me, who can be against me?" (see Romans 8:31) began to make sense. I am created to live *in* this world. To love *in* this world. To be wholeheartedly *alive* right here and right now. Unafraid, unbound, and untethered to the fear of man. Unafraid, unbound, and untethered to the fear of not being enough.

You have been perfectly intended to fulfill His purpose in this world. You were created by Him, and created for courage, confidence, and brilliance. This liberation is rooted in the fundamental belief that God's love for mankind (and thus, our unmerited but inherent worth) will birth confidence that will grow into a universal awareness—both a self-awareness *and* an others-awareness.

Liberation that is built on this leveling belief of God's love and purpose for *all* mankind frees not only our own selves from the incessant desire to please others, but also frees others to live their own life's story.

When we are confident in who we are and in our own

life's story and brilliance, then we are also okay when others' lives do not look like our own. If you've been liberated from others' expectations, then *they also* have been liberated from the expectations that *you* were possibly placing on them! Because if you can be confident based on the belief that "God is for me," then you must recognize that others are able to be confident in their *own* unique lives, because God is also *for them*!

In short? Liberation breeds liberation. Confidence breeds confidence. Self-awareness built upon the truth of human nature and the redemptive love of God will breed others-awareness.

We begin to see the beautiful application of this collective liberation when we receive and give the ol' benefit of the doubt. We see it when we treat one another as if we don't know everything about them. When we begin to see them as wonderfully unique individuals, then they no longer threaten our sense of self-worth—and so we can stop running from them and stop trying to squeeze them into our idea of what they "should" look like. We see this liberation when we understand that we exist to display collaboration, not competition. Unity, not uniformity. And when this application takes hold in our hearts, then dehumanizing someone else to the point of telling them to go kill themselves when they don't make a play...well, that doesn't happen anymore. Because when we are liberated by God's love, and we allow others to be liberated to be who they are, we put ourselves in their shoes. We humanize one another. We have empathy and compassion for one another and we realize the celebrity we are so quick to judge is a human being with a real heart that aches and dreams and loves deeply. We see the baseball player as being an actual human being and maybe an amazing father or even the husband of the woman sitting right next to you.

AUTHORITY AUDITIONS

Sometimes it takes a daydream to open your eyes.

The minute your eyes are wide open, you become aware of your own heart and the heart authority you have inherently been given. When you become self-aware that your heart authority is God's and God's alone, then you can really understand that you have been given implicit value and worth because He made you. When you operate out of the fundamental belief that you are loved, then that heart authority will establish a heart filter (the truth of God's promises found in His Word) that is strong enough to sift out the other things in life that will fight for your heart authority.

Suddenly, when fear tries to take hold in that tender heart of yours—fear of what you or others might think, or do, or say, or feel—your heart filter will keep that out. Because if God is for you, who can be against you (Romans 8:31)? If He is in your corner, why be afraid (Psalm 1:18)? Use that fear to motivate you to keep moving forward. Shut the fear down by doing exactly what it is telling you you cannot do. Let the heart authority of God's divine love for you help you choose the corn snake over the teddy bear. God has given you a road map and a filter that show you His commandments and promises. He has promised *never* to leave you or forsake you. You are safe in Him.

When other people are vying for your heart authority in order to try to control you—trying to *should* on you— don't be easily swayed. Instead, answer with, "Don't *should* on me!" Don't allow them to become your authority. That belongs only to God and what *He* says about you: that you are loved; you are intended; you have been given a conscience and a brain to make decisions for your own life, within the protective bounds of Scripture.

When someone is attempting to use verbal gymnastics to control you, suddenly you can recognize how easily you begin to walk on eggshells in that relationship when you are not honest. Be honest in the way you communicate. The truth will set you free. Don't allow yourself to succumb to the desire for self-protection at the expense of honesty. Your true heart authority is who God says you are. His words are the words to listen to. Believing you are worthy and intended and wholly loved by God will keep you from being controlled by others' words, and will make you strong, firm, and steadfast.

With eyes wide open, I look around the stadium and see 50,000 beating hearts. Some pitter-patter with overwhelming love for the person they are thinking of. Some ache, feeling the pangs of judgment or the pains of invalidation. Some beat faster with hurt from others' words. I see them in syncopated rhythm—*dadum, dadum, dadum*. I do a 360 and I see the man with the jersey and the Bud Light. The hurtful, offensive, rude, aggressive man I want to despise because he spoke ugly words against the man I love.

But, with eyes wide open, I see him for what he really is: *Approved*.

PART

IDENTITY

TWO

THE IMAGE AND IDENTITY MIX-UP

"UGLY" SILVER JACKET

Standing in my closet is like standing in the middle of a life-sized Crayola box, every color of the rainbow represented, all in their respective ROYGBIV groupings.

Well, red is out. The Cleveland Indians are red and all I need is to show up at Wrigley Field in the opposing team's colors, we lose the series, and I become the infamous new Billy Goat. Goodness knows, there is no room for error here.

The second factor in my closet conundrum is the TV. You've all heard that TV makes you gain ten pounds, right? Well, it does. So, my normal androgynous, oversized style needed to take a bit more of a tailored turn.

I spotted a silver collar. My husband had gotten the jacket for me for my birthday. I had been pregnant when he gave it to me. It was one of those "someday" outfits that served as a sort of depressing motivational postdelivery inspiration to get back to my prebaby weight. I tried it on for the first time since having my daughter. It fit! It felt like the right choice since Benny had gotten it for me, so I donned the jacket with its discombobulated black threading, a big ruffle on the left-side pocket, and four holes for buttons but only three buttons, making the jacket look uneven at the bottom. (You know when you realize you missed a button and everything is out of alignment? That.) But it was on purpose. Subversive design humor. *So* me.

I stepped into my jeans and buttoned up the jacket. With a flip of my head, I shook out my crimped hair, courtesy of my 1980s-era crimper that gives me the platinum Afro look I love. Blue velvet heels? Obviously. With a look and a nod in my floor-length mirror, I skipped down the stairs to greet my family, who had just arrived. Between two vehicles and two Ubers, we made our way to the stadium.

My nerves were getting the best of me as I followed a security guard through the concourse. You see, today I was singing "God Bless America" at game four of THE WORLD SERIES. Worse, the Cubs hadn't won the World Series in 108 years because of the notorious Curse of the Billy Goat. Maximum-level nerves. Though I tend to take my time hitting the mark stylistically on a pretty regular basis, this day it was particularly important to get the outfit *just* right.

With Blaise on my hip, Kruse holding my left hand, and Zion walking on my right, I was grateful for the needed distraction they brought.

The security guard took a sharp left turn down into a tunnel that led out onto the grass, right next to the ivy outfield wall. Even though it was over an hour before the first pitch would be thrown, there wasn't an unclaimed seat in the stadium. As fans yelled at me over the railing, some shouting words of excitement and some just shouting *at* me, I tightened my hold on the kids and kept close to my assigned security guard. We walked by the dugout and I glanced in to see if Ben was there, but he was still in the clubhouse. Fortunately, that silver jacket Ben gave me was hugging me tight, and I felt a warmth and a confidence settle in, as if he were standing right beside me. I'd made the right choice. A few more steps and we reached the dirt behind home plate. I sighed as I put Blaise down.

I took a few pictures with fans through the net, then began to get my ears set and mind focused. I thought about my younger sister, an officer in the Coast Guard, about her commitment to our country and her sacrifice to serve in ways that most are completely unaware of. I prayed as I walked in between the pitcher's mound and home plate to perform.

I sang, trying to soak it all in and hold tight to that feeling of immense gratitude. But in less than two minutes, the moment was over. The crowd applauded. I took a breath. I waved. I smiled to the camera. I smiled at Ben, who was standing on the third base line. God bless America.

I sat down with the rest of my family. After Ben's at-bat, I leaned over to my older sister. "I need a water, want anything?" I said.

I made my way down to the concessions and joined the long, winding line. I noticed the man standing behind me, probably in his midforties, wearing a nondescript collared red shirt. Cubs fan or Indians fan? Who knows! And that, folks, is why I didn't wear red. Better to not be on anyone's side than look like you're on both sides equally.

I could hear the man talking quietly to his friend in the line next to us. My guess was that they were trying to see which line would move faster (I do it all the time), but this provided just enough distance that I could overhear their quiet whispers. Finally his friend said, "Well, just ask her!"

"Aren't you Julianna Zobrist?" Red Shirt Man asked.

"Yes," I said with little inflection, unsure of where this was going.

"Wow. You have such a phenomenal voice! Really, we were just saying that it was the best version of 'God Bless America' we have ever heard!"

"Well, thank you!"

"Yeah!" the friend of Red Shirt Man chimed in, clearly unable to handle what was in his boozy cup. "You were *so* good. But we were wondering…'cause you're, you know…hot…why d'you dress so ugly?" Red Shirt Man shot his friend a look and I went bug-eyed. I have a terrible poker face and typically laugh when I get uncomfortable. Not catching Red Shirt Man's clue, the friend continued. "Well, dude, *you're* the one who said 'she could be so much prettier if she didn't dress so ugly.'"

I tried to remain cool and not show them that I was completely repulsed. "Well, lucky for y'all, I don't care what you think." I smiled and let out an uncomfortable laugh as I turned away and ordered my water. *Finally!*

As I walked back to my seat, I thought about an incident that happened three weeks earlier. I'd done a live interview where the audience could chime in with any questions they had. We talked about identity and self-expression and empowerment. One woman (in a slightly passive-aggressive tone...my favorite, you know) asked me, "How can you feel good about yourself, talking to women about identity, and yet you dye your hair?"

Okay...

"Well, first of all, I don't *dye* my hair; I bleach my hair." The audience laughed—so did I, uncomfortably, of course. "But secondly, and most important, I think you're misunderstanding what I mean when I talk about identity."

Thus began a conversation about the difference between image and identity. One I have continued to explore within the confines of my own life and in the bigger picture of what that means in an existential way. Who am I? What do I believe about myself? How am I perceived? What do words like *identity* and *image* even mean?

Ah, sweet semantics.

PORTRAIT OF AN ARTIST AS AN ARTIST

The *Arnolfini Portrait* is one of those paintings that everyone swears they've never heard of until they see it. *Oh. Thaaat one! The one with the pregnant lady wearing the green dress. Yeah. Got it.*

But that little somber painting is in my top ten for sure.

It's rich with detail and is a fantastic example of the oil paintings from the Northern Renaissance era. To some, it may look like just another straightforward family portrait. However, the *Arnolfini* is one of Western art history's greatest riddles—and you would never know it if you didn't have just the right amount of context.

Two figures stand in a small room with a bed on the right and a window on the left. They pose formally, and even by painting standards, they are very still. On the left, a man stares ahead, wearing a weighty coat and a hat. His right hand is raised. His left hand is limply and weirdly holding a lady's hand. The lady looks very sad. And very pregnant.

But surprise—she most certainly is not!

It was actually fashionable at the time to look pregnant. Some might say it was faking the harvest to attract the seed, while others say it was because the more cloth a merchant's wife wore, the wealthier she appeared. (And people say a silver jacket is weird?)

But there is an even more important thing to note than fashion trends when it comes to this unique little painting. Behind the man and woman is an ornate Latin signature that translates as "Jan van Eyck was here 1434." If, like me, you're thinking of middle school bathroom stalls or subway graffiti, you are not wrong and that is no accident. It was the artist's signature to inscribe his pictures in witty ways. Underneath the inscription is a mirror and in that mirror are not only the backs of the man and woman, but two additional figures, one of whom most likely is the artist himself.

My point? Art is always a self-portrait of the artist. Here we have van Eyck's own image reflected in his creation. But even if there was no identifiable figure in that mirror, he would still be present. The symbolism that flows from the imagery reveals a mind rich with images and poetry and witticisms, and thus we get a good idea of what he could be like. But just a small piece.

So, if the art itself is an image, the identity of that art is found in the artist.

Image = amazing Northern Renaissance oil painting

Identity = van Eyck

Image = kooky clothes and bleached hair

Identity = Julianna Zobrist

Because identity, to me, is who you are on the inside—who you intrinsically are. Heaven forbid our identity is limited to our images, because if our image, specifically our hair (as the woman in the audience was suggesting), is our identity, then what does that say about the person with bad hair? What does it say about the woman who looks pregnant because she's wearing a really fashionable dress according to the Netherlands style in the fifteenth century? Does it mean because she *looks* pregnant that she is with child? Um, no. If it is true that our image is our identity, then what does that mean for the identity of an infant, born *without* hair? Does the infant have no identity until he or she has an appropriate (what does that even mean) image? The logic is preposterous and laughable.

But let's go medieval for a minute and say that the ability to change our image really does hold weight in our identity. Then every time you dye (or bleach) your hair, every time you put on makeup, every time you get your nails done, every time you go to the gym and get a little stronger, every time you force your butt into Spanx, you have somehow changed your identity. Do all of these things change our image? Yes! But our identity cannot be found in our ever-fluctuating and always-changing image. And thank the good Lord for that, because heaven help me I will not give up my Spanx!

One thing everybody who knows me understands is that I *love* fashion. I love how it makes me feel and how I am able to express myself with all the colors of the rainbow (and most of the time all at once). So, image, if understood, can be a really beautiful thing. Self-expression is often a huge part of understanding the larger identity of who someone is. If you wear a silver jacket with a lot of asymmetric detailing and some wacky threads, then you might like the idea of taking convention and flipping it on its head. You might be a rule breaker. You might be a little more rebellious. That's awesome. If you wear a

T-shirt with your favorite sports team, you might be loyal. You might like to be a part of a larger community. You may love the idea of representation and celebrations and union. That's awesome too. If you put on a shirt because it's clean and you had nothing else to wear and don't really care, you may just have other interests and priorities, and I love that too.

My silver jacket was an opportunity to express myself, sure, but it was also the idea of wearing a gift that my man gave me on a night that was special for both of us. If Red Shirt Man knew that, then maybe he would have kept his mouth shut and not have called something so symbolic to me "ugly." As I regularly tell my children: "You don't have to like it; you just need to appreciate it."

The *Arnolfini Portrait* was an opportunity for van Eyck to express *himself*. It was crazy symbolic to him. When you look at that image, it is pregnant (no pun intended) with symbolism. The dog represents fidelity. The mirror is God's all-seeing eye. And, no, not everyone needs to *like* the painting, but everybody needs to *appreciate* it.

So, when we start to understand and get context as to what someone's image represents, it starts to reveal something about our identity in a larger sense.

IMAGE BEARERS

Now let's get to the good part.

We are all walking *Arnolfini Portrait*s.

We bear the image of our Creator deep inside us in myriad symbolic little ways.

We see it when we love. We see it when we create. We see it when we empathize. And the minute we realize that our Creator's identity is found deep inside us and is inscribed on our very hearts is the minute we start to understand who we truly are.

Imago Dei.

We are made in the image of God.

In the same way that van Eyck made an image of himself in that painting, and that painting can find its identity in its creator, so God made us in His image. The context makes the whole thing way more beautiful (both for the painting and, ya know, for humanity's entire existence).

I believe that our true identity is in the fact that *we* (meaning all humankind) were made in *God's* image. We identify in God's image, not our own. Scripture says, "So God created man in his own image, in the image of God he created him; male and female he created them" (Genesis 1:27 NIV).

Image, as defined by Webster's Dictionary:

> *: a reproduction or imitation of the form of a person or thing; especially: an imitation in solid form.*
>
> *: the optical counterpart of an object produced by an optical device such as a lens or mirror*
>
> *: a visual representation of something*[1]

Usually, when I think of the word *image*, it is in the context of what we wear and what we look like and how we are perceived. Yes, image can definitely be a visual representation of our creativity, our likes and dislikes. But I love the definition that defines image as "an imitation in solid form"—which makes me think immediately of something beautiful that C. S. Lewis, the acclaimed Christian apologist and author, explored in *Mere Christianity*:

A statue has the shape of a man but is not alive. In the same way, man has (in a sense I am going to explain) the "shape" or likeness of God, but he has not got the kind of life God has. Let us take the first point (man's resemblance to God) first. Everything God has made has some likeness to Himself. Space is like Him in its hugeness: not that the greatness of space is the same kind of greatness as God's, but it is a sort of symbol of it, or a translation of it into non-spiritual terms. Matter is like God in having energy: though, again, of course, physical energy is a different kind of thing from the power of God. The vegetable world is like Him because it is alive, and He is the "living God." But life, in this biological sense, is not the same as the life there is in God: it is only a kind of symbol or shadow of it.[2]

Growing up, I would have considered myself a naturalist. With respect to human nature, evolution, and biology, I felt such awe in the things I would observe. I had no other appropriate word to describe its origin than to call it God. Just as I would write songs and poetry to reflect myself, I saw all of creation, its beauty and function and intentionality, as a reflection of God Himself. So, if beauty and function and intentionality of creation are all born out of the design of a creator, then understanding our Creator is of utmost importance to understanding ourselves (and, thus, our identity).

Genesis 1:26 (NASB) tells us we were created in the image of God: "Then God said, 'Let us make man in our image, after our likeness. And let them have dominion over the fish of the sea and over the birds of the heavens and over the livestock and over all the earth and over every creeping thing that creeps on the earth.'"

Jump to 1 John 4:8 (NIV), which says, "Anyone who does not love does not know God, because God is love."

God is love.

Because God is love and because out of this motivation of love He has created you and me and all things, then that means that you and I were created with the intention and purpose of love. If we get to identify in the image of God as His creation, instead of the image of ourselves (and how awesome or not awesome our hair is), then we get to identify in His attributes. So, in many ways that means that *we* are love.

Genesis 1:31 (NIV) says, "God saw all that He had made and it was very good." If a painter deems his painting of the utmost value, then that painting has intrinsic value. That's just the way art works. The value and worth of something created is really estimated by its creator. I believe you have intrinsic value. That you and I have implicit value and worth...not because we have mustered up some way to be impressive to ourselves, to one another, or to our Creator, but because our capital C Creator gave us implicit value and worth and love.

Psalm 139 (ESV) contains some of my favorite verses about God's thoughts of us:

> For you formed my inward parts; you knitted me together in my mother's womb. I praise you, for I am fearfully and wonderfully made. Wonderful are your works; my soul knows it very well. My frame was not hidden from you, when I was being made in the secret, intricately woven in the depths of the earth. Your eyes saw my unformed substance; in your book were written, every one of them, the days that were formed for me, when as yet there was none of them. How precious to me are your thoughts, O God! How vast is the sum of them! If I would count them, they are more than the sand. I awake, and I am still with you.

Your frame was not hidden from God as you were being created. He knew your frame; He knew what you would look like, the number of hairs on your head. He knew you as intimately as an artist knows the detail and precision it requires to paint a certain part of his portrait. You are a reflection of God Himself—intrinsically valuable, worthy, and loved.

When you believe this, and champion this for all mankind, you are freed to be okay with yourself and, in turn, be okay with others being different from you. Just as I knew the designer of that silver jacket and decided to put on what they made, so, too, we must know our Designer and decide to "put on" His attributes. When we do this, we are able to have the same kind of appreciation for ourselves—as intrinstically valuable, worthy, and loved—as we have upon entering the doors of the National Gallery in London where we're met with immensely beautiful and diverse paintings, sculptures, and drawings. Just as you would admire the paintings and praise the painters, we, too, should admire our Creator's creation and praise Him for His immensely beautiful and good works.

I believe that in the midst of this beautiful collaboration of different images and creative self-expressions, we can be unified in this fact: *You and I were made in God's image, and it is very good.*

7

THE FIVE O'CLOCK GLASS
OF PINOT

OF EXISTENTIAL CRISES AND
SPLINTERS

For some strange, cosmic reason, every time I was in the process of releasing a record, I would find out I was pregnant. Three records, three kids, y'all. I'm not making this up.

I vividly remember recording the video shoot for *Shatterproof* while being four months pregnant. It was an all-day shoot and I had to plan not just my looks for the various songs, but my snack breaks as well. I'm one of those lucky throw-up-till-you're-five-months-along pregnant girls. I would arrive at the studio with one babe on my hip and the other holding my hand. There were several times that midsong, I would need to take a break to get a snack or to throw up in the small bathroom at the corner of the stage.

Staring at my reflection in that porcelain throne, I would think, *Why in heaven's name do you keep doing this to yourself, Jules?*

Once baby number three entered the world, I traveled all over supporting my husband's career with one kid on my hip, one holding my hand, and another in the stroller, while still trying to keep my dream alive, writing music until the wee hours.

It was exhausting.

Is this uncharted territory or is this illegal trespassing? Am I even cut out for this? The self-doubt and uncertainty left me yelling at the top of my lungs. This lack of life direction propelled me to Google things like "purpose," "a woman's purpose," and "someone tell me Julianna Zobrist's purpose in life please and thank you."

February rolled around, and we had just made our yearly move down to Phoenix, Arizona, for spring training. In a rental home, with a brand-new three-month-old, my four-year-old daughter, seven-year-old son, and no friends or family around, I was afraid of becoming what I had vowed I would *never* become: the resentful mother with nothing going on for herself who hangs out in her sweats all day and lives for her five o'clock glass of pinot noir.

Yet, there I was, in my sweatpants with a glass of rosé at noon. (I had timed it that I wouldn't have to nurse again for another three hours, so all you ladies freaking out can get your panties out of a wad now.) I was sitting on an overstuffed white linen sofa that was overdressed by the eight cream-colored satin throw pillows lined in formation against the back cushion. A large glass-top coffee table with brass legs rested on the white shag carpet. To my right, a somber, neutral-colored watercolor print hung in solitude on the wall. To my left, a fake palm tree branch loomed over my shoulder. Basically, the antithesis of my own personal Crayola box interior-design style.

I'd ordered some books that had arrived earlier that day, so I restlessly cracked one open. Books on womanhood, a woman's purpose, the purpose of women, a girl's purpose... you get the idea. Some of them were from a generalized worldview and some were specifically geared toward Christian women. Five pages of notes later, I began to see a common thread throughout what I was reading. Our femininity and womanhood are apparently defined by being a mother, a wife, or a maid. Female existence can be boiled down to how well we juggle domestic roles and duties.

A small cry brought my head up and out of the books.

My three-month-old was awake from her nap. I went into the next room and picked her up from her crib. I stood there for a few minutes, rocking her peacefully back and forth, while still mulling over the things I had been reading. I changed her diaper, then sat back down on the couch to nurse her. With my feet propped up on the glass coffee table and the Boppy in place, I fed my baby and continued reading and studying.

Another cry.

This time it came from my four-year-old daughter. Kruse had been out in the backyard playing on the swing set and got a splinter in her hand.

After asking her to grab my tweezers from the bathroom because I couldn't get up right then with Blaise, I tried to take the splinter out of her hand. As I was simultaneously reading, writing, nursing my infant, and working to get the splinter out of my wiggly little chick's hand, I had an unanticipated thought burst into my brain like someone had yanked open the curtains in a pitch-dark room.

Wait a minute.

She's a girl, I thought in my head, still holding on to my little one's hand.

"And so are you," I whispered, glancing down at my youngest.

And if these books are right, then *neither* of my little girls has a purpose yet.

Neither of them are married, neither of them have babies of their own, neither of them have a home to manage, neither of them have someone else to mentor…shoot, neither of them can read and one of them can't even speak yet.

Mind. Blown.

The ghastly implications being taught in these books kept unraveling before my eyes. What if my girls never do get married? Lord knows I'd love me some grandbabies someday, but what if neither of my girls can even have babies? What if they never have a family of their own? Are they choosing no purpose if they choose not to marry? What if one of my girls gets married but then her husband leaves her? Or, God forbid, what if she loses a child? Does her life become void of purpose if it becomes void of these roles? It began to dawn on me that *purpose*, as defined by these books, was something subject to our ability to fulfill various roles. Either that, *or...*

These books are full of bull.

THE F-WORD

It was a manifesto. Then a philosophical category. Then a movement. Then a slur. And now, the F-word is back, worn on trendy T-shirts and front and center in the ever-elusive social-media bio: *feminism*.

Worry not, I'm not about to dive into some already flooded, diluted, and muddied waters here because my stance is pretty darn straightforward.

I am a woman.

And, yes, I am pro-women. I love women and how we are unique from men. I love my femininity.

However, I am also pro-men. I love men and what the men in my life have brought to the world. I have a son and am so unbelievably pro his future, just as I am fighting for my daughters. Likewise, I would fight for my husband's rights just as I would fight for my own. Equality. I do not believe the future is female. I believe the future is female and male...a future that must grow from a common ground of humanity characterized by love and empathy and understanding and compassion and bravery and redemption.

I keep my opinion wide-ranging to lessen the common risk of oversimplification when it comes to the roles of women *and* men. Women are obviously meant for more than baby and sandwich making. Men are obviously meant for more than doing bench presses, bringing home the bacon, and keeping their emotions at a distance. It sounds obvious, but it's still the way we tend to treat gender norms—whether we even know it or not. The truth is, we are doing it to others and we subconsciously are doing it to ourselves too.

This is what I realized as I took the Enneagram Test a few months ago. Actually, I took it three times. (That tells you something about my personality type, I'm sure.) My highest score was type Eight, the Challenger, and my very close second was type Three, the Achiever. (For those of you who are familiar with the Enneagram Institute, that will make sense to you, but for those of you who are not familiar, I highly recommend taking the test.) As I scrolled through the descriptions, what I found extremely interesting was a disclaimer that popped up as I was reading about how to interpret the various types. It was called "Misidentification."

"If you are a woman and your Two score is highest, look at your next two high scores—women are often taught to play the role of the Two whether it is their basic type or not."

Type Two is "the Helper."

Here's the official description: "We have named personality type Two *The Helper* because people of this type are either the most genuinely helpful to other people or, when they are less healthy they are the most highly invested in *seeing themselves* as helpful. Being generous and going out of their way for others makes Twos feel that theirs is the richest, most meaningful way to live. The love and concern they feel—and the genuine good they do—warms their hearts and makes them feel worthwhile. Twos are most interested in what they feel to be the 'really, really good' things in life—love, closeness, sharing, family and friendship."[1]

One of my dearest friends is a type Two. She is intrinsically helpful and sincere. She is a special needs teacher, always looking to cook for others, and has a heart for service and hosting that is unlike most I've met. I, on the other hand, called Ben on the phone a week before we got married and said facetiously, "Hello, my name is Julianna Gilmore. I really hope you realize that you are marrying *me* and not someone else. You see, I hate cooking. Oh, I'll do it so that we don't starve, but I cook healthy and bland. This is not going to be some sort of three-course-casserole-dinner-with-a-dessert-daily situation for you. But, hey, I can pick up dinner from Whole Foods like a boss."

Though I didn't realize it at the time, I was battling against the unspoken expectations of femininity that I, and most likely culture, had placed upon myself. As "the big day" crept closer and closer, it was as if I were stepping closer and closer to the ultimate *Mona Lisa* of "femininity" and "biblical womanhood," a portrait that I knew I wasn't going to live up to.

Step by step, as the portrait became clearer and clearer before me, I began to realize just how vastly different I looked from it. How vastly different I had been created. And the phone call to my fiancé that evening was the desperate plea of "Do you still want me, even though I am different from what the ultimate picture of femininity portrays? Will you still love me if I never know how to make a lasagna from scratch? Does God approve of this style of womanhood?"

Ultimately, *Am I okay just being me?*

See, when we attach specific actions and roles like cooking, cleaning, relying on a man to bring in the income, and staying at home to something as fundamental as being feminine or masculine, we alienate those who are not living by those specific definitions. That leads to pride. Which leads to division. Which leads to using sloppy theology to tether our roles to our purpose. We overstereotype and oversimplify and overgeneralize to a point where we do not belong if we do not fit into this mold called "femininity." Or worse, we feel that something is *wrong*.

Remember back in kindergarten when you were asked what you wanted to be when you grow up? I always answered that I wanted to be a forensic scientist and a singer. Yeah, sure, I might need counseling for the whole right brain–left brain conundrum I've got going on, but my vision was set. I don't remember any little girl saying, "When I grow up, I want to do the dishes every night and watch TV and drink a glass of pinot noir to fall asleep." Likewise, I never knew a young boy to say, "I want to work all day at a desk from nine to five and come home to watch golf and have some scotch."

That's because this is not a gender versus gender issue. This is a people-deciding-to-get-off-their-butt-and-do-what-they-need-to-do-for-their-own-life issue. This is a people-not-letting-their-identity-be-grounded-in-what-society-thinks-it-should-be issue.

God has a universal dream for His sons and daughters, and it is bigger than our narrow interpretations or small constructions of manhood and womanhood (or feminism, for that matter). It's bigger than frozen-in-time arguments or cultural biases, bigger than marital status or birth rate. Bigger than trendy political movements.

DOMESTICITY SHOWDOWN

Jesus and His disciples are headed to Jerusalem, and on the way, they stop and are welcomed into the home of two lovely sisters, Martha and Mary.

We can imagine Martha scurrying about—getting enough clean plates out of the dishwasher (maybe even bringing out the "good" china), ensuring that clean hand towels are in the guest bathroom, spritzing some lavender spray in the air, casually throwing together a gourmet meal, smiling and graciously greeting everyone.

Out of the corner of her eye she sees Mary, sitting at the feet of Jesus in the posture of a rabbi's pup. *Geez, so unhelpful.*

Finally, a bit frazzled, she lets off some steam and re-minds Jesus of Mary's domestic duties and responsibility to tending to the other guests: "Lord, do you not care that my sister has left me to do all the work by myself? Tell her then to help me." Jesus answers, "Martha, Martha, you are worried and distracted by many things; there is need of only one thing. Mary has chosen the better part, which will not be taken away from her" (see Luke 10:38–42).

The problem was not that one woman wanted to have a nice dinner and one woman wanted to learn. I totally get it! Sometimes you just need a little help with the meal prep. I sympathize with Martha wanting to put a nice plate of food in front of Jesus. I mean, He *is* the Messiah, so no pressure, right? But the problem in this situation was that one sister *criticized* the other for not being domestic. Judging another woman's domesticity (or lack thereof) or your own idea of femininity will only hin-der you from owning your own life and the decisions you have made for yourself and will create a sinkhole of com-petition and confinement in your relationships.

Mary prioritized the opportunity to learn over an an-cient idea of femininity, and Jesus honored that choice: As some translations state, "She chose the better way."

It's important to note that people in the first century normally sat on chairs during a meal. Mary's act of sitting at the feet of Jesus was uniquely the place of a disciple. More specifically, it was the place of a student learning from a rabbi. In other words, that was a big ol' cultural no-no. For Mary to forgo her expected role as a woman—that is, making sandwiches—she would have been committing a reasonably shocking act.

Guys, this is classic cultural subversion and *I love it*. Jesus was empowering women to rise up and engage with culture. To challenge norms and eventually be prepared for when the time came for those norms to be squashed. He was inviting women (and men) to choose intentionality over conventional expectations. He was enticing us all with a life well lived, saying, "Hey, ditch the idea of obligation for obligation's sake and live the most fulfilling life you possibly can!"

JUST DO IT

I get a lot of people side-eyeing and telling me what a good mother would do. Surprise, surprise.

And guess what? Sure, I don't **need** to work. I could 100 percent be a stay-at-home mama and I would love it. But, for me, it has always been about a few other things: investment, creativity, confidence.

I've always wanted to know what I am capable of. I never want to lose confidence in my own intrinsic self-expression. I never want to lose sight of *me*. I've always believed that God is present in each of us and there are glimpses of who He is in the various different ways we express ourselves.

Right now, I am sitting on my bright blue sofa while my kids do their schoolwork. My husband is at the field about to play a baseball game in two hours. I have been sitting at my laptop writing and researching for the last three hours. I just picked up my phone to text my friend who invited me to go shopping with her that I won't be able to make it. I've got one more hour of writing to do. I will pick up my laptop again at 4:00 a.m. so that I can write from 4:00 to 6:00 a.m. without being interrupted. It's not always fun, but it is always fulfilling.

Deciding to invest in yourself isn't made easier by what is convenient. Investing in yourself happens when you decide that it is *worth* it! Worth the time, worth the harassment from your friends for never having seen the latest TV show, worth the lack of sleep, worth the sweat, worth the tears, worth the scrutiny you are sure to receive when you release your creativity to the world. It's worth taking the *should*s that you will be pressured with and being brave enough to tell them to shove it.

Is it worth it to you to miss that nap during the day so that you can take your online course and, ultimately, earn your degree? Is it worth it to you to say no to going out with friends so that you can use that money you would have spent to rent out a studio next month? Is it worth it to say no to the chips and *queso* at lunch because you want to lose those extra twelve pounds? Is it worth skipping that five o'clock cocktail on the couch to paint a portrait?

What is your investment worth to you? That is a question only you can answer. Either way, it's high time that we begin to see and believe in our capability to invest in ourselves. It's high time we stop whining about our lives. In my case, I'm not as good a cook as other women are, and so I either need to take some cooking classes or decide for *myself* that those classes aren't *worth* the time to me, therefore *owning* the fact that my meals are simple. I *own* the fact that I prioritize writing over being a culinary master.

When you begin to value the *investment* more than the *becoming*, I believe you are able to enjoy the process of those in-between times—the times of losing some much-needed sleep to cram in a few more hours of doing something you really love.

So, here's the spoiler: I didn't grow up to become a successful singing forensic scientist with a culinary degree, but I have made the sacrifices I've needed to make to pursue music and writing. And, yes, I am a mom to three irreplaceable kids and I sacrifice time I could be investing in music and writing so that I can try to be the absolute best mom that I can be. And, yes, I did turn down an important meeting last week so I could have a date night with my man. And *that* to me is profound purpose. *That* to me is investing in myself.

So now that you know it, go do it. Own that decision and value it. And stop concerning yourself with other women and men who make decisions you would not make. If you want twenty kids and you're able, *do it*. If you want to be the editor in chief at a fashion magazine, *you can do that too*. Do you want to pick up your paintbrush again that has been dry since college? Maybe shut off the TV during your baby's naptime and pull out a canvas. Why not take that writing class you've always wanted to take? Or tuck those sugary munchkins in at night and get in the bath, light some candles, and read a book (don't forget the glass of pinot noir). Shoot, if you want, take the glass of pinot to the foot of Jesus with you. Thanks to Mary's teaching, you can do that too! Ultimately, things like feminism and success are about being okay with the choices you make.

Remember, what is best for you is between you and God.

8
SPIRITUAL BOTOX

PIXELS AND PERFECTION

I woke up early Friday morning, carefully crawling out of bed so that I wouldn't wake my sleep-deprived husband. Tiptoeing quickly across the room and into the bathroom, I shut the door before turning on the light, trying not to let a giggle slip out amidst my excitement that kept me up throughout the night. Today was the photo shoot for my record and I could not be more ready. It had taken months of planning and preparation in anticipation of this day. I had styled nine looks and twelve setups that were specifically designed for the twelve tracks on the record. Everything was thoughtful, intentional, and mapped out to a tee. I drank two bottles of water (as is my morning routine before doing anything else) and then picked up my toothbrush. As I began brushing my teeth, I looked in the mirror for the first time. My toothbrush came to a screeching halt as I let out a gasp. What. The. Heck. Is. That?

It was a big one.

Not a mild one. Not an under-the-skin one. Not in the hair line or somewhere inconspicuous. But on my freaking cheek. A white to pinkish red mountain of hormones just begging to erupt. Yes, erupt. It was a volcanic entity so big, it deserved a name. Velma. Velma the Volcano.

An hour later, I rolled up to the studio where we would be shooting that day. I saw my makeup artist across the room, already setting up her station and lights and my makeup chair. *"You're going to love this!"* I yelled sarcastically as I walked through a maze of cameras and crew members, trying not to trip on the massive cords running along the floor.

"Oh wow," she said.

"I know." We both just shook our heads and took a moment of silence to reflect on the science experiment on my face.

A couple hours later, we were done with glam and went over the schedule for the day with the entire team. Everything was ready, everyone was prepared, and music was pumping through the sound system. Everything went better than planned. The only hitch was the shadow that was going to be on my cheek in every single photo.

"No worries; we will just fix that in post," my photographer said.

"Post" is the work that is done after the photos are

taken. The images are in digital form and someone very detail-oriented and very talented goes pixel by pixel, fixing the imperfect things on an imperfect face. In this case, the one and only Velma the Volcano. And sure enough, a week later, after the photo shoot was done and we had time to look through raw images and choose which ones we wanted to have edited, Velma had been vanquished from the photographs. And I was not mad about that at all.

That's the thing about editing in post. It's not reality. The reality was the living organism on my face, but pixel by pixel, it had been edited out to perfection. I was made up of little bitty flesh-colored squares. Photoshop is like digital Botox—except it lasts forever.

What is it about humanity that keeps multibillion-dollar industries alive, based solely on our desire to attempt to perfect imperfectability? Is there even the possibility of being a human who is able to avoid the desire to correct?

THE YOUNG AND THE RESTLESS

Turn on the TV in your living room. Glance at the magazines and tabloids while waiting in line at the grocery store. Look up at the billboards as you stroll through downtown. Scroll through your newsfeed while waiting for your coffee.

Everywhere you look you'll see something we cultivate in our culture. It's difficult to resist and it's reinforced ubiquitously. These cultural messages feed the deepest insecurities in ourselves and encourage us to believe we must be something different from who we really are. We hold ourselves to an impossible standard: perfection.

Enter modern day's real-life Photoshop: botulinum toxin.

I'm sure you've all heard of Botox and the (sometimes accurate) stereotype of how Botox prevents your face from moving and you become an expressionless human mannequin with perfectly smooth skin. Oddly enough, this magical toxin that millions inject into their face regularly is hands-down one of *the* most toxic poisons known to science. In fact, just a gram could kill a million people. But due to the judicious supervision of modern-day health care, rather than knock you out, it just causes a bit of paralysis of the muscles.

How does it work, you ask?   •

Muscles are triggered to clench up or contract by nerve signals. The nerve and the muscle are separated by a small gap (the neuromuscular junction). The nerve releases a chemical messenger called *acetylcholine* into the gap, the acetylcholine sticks to the muscle, and the muscle contracts. Basically, Botox stops the nerve from being able to release acetylcholine. Without acetylcholine, there's no way for the nerve to communicate with the muscle, so the muscle becomes paralyzed.[1]

Bibbidi Bobbidi Boo. Every wrinkle corrected. Every blemish gone. Perfection achieved!

But here's the thing about this fairy-tale botulinum toxin: The effects start appearing a few days after injections, reach a maximum after around two weeks, and last around three to five months. That's it. Not even half a year will pass before you will again find yourself in that sterile, fluorescently saturated white room with a needle in your face.

So, while pixels are fake and everlasting, Botox is real but temporary.

The point? Chasing perfection is chasing the unattainable. You'll either end up always hiding behind the figurative pixelated mask or trying to keep up with your own fallibility in an endless pursuit of correction.

It's easy to get swept up by the fear that we just aren't enough. We think we aren't pretty enough, smart enough, or *good* enough—but how do we balance those expectations of whatever being "good enough" means with the reality of our humanity?

When reality hits and we walk outside into the real world with Velma front and center or the aftereffects of the injectable fades away, how do we come to terms with the fact that we are human and therefore imperfectable?

Well, I've got some good news for you.

I believe our bent toward perfection is not so simply explained by vanity or self-obsession. That would be way too easy. Oh, sure, perfection is much more easily written off, excused, and ignored by the shrug of "She's so vain," but I believe our bent toward perfection is much more complex than that. I believe this is a bent toward heaven. A bent toward the divine. A bent toward the only perfect perfectable. God Himself.

I don't think there is even a *possibility* of being human

and avoiding this inclination to correct. I believe we have all been given restless heavenly souls that live in imperfect human bodies. Therein lies the explanation behind why we want to correct. Why we want to dress in a way that maybe covers the scar on our leg. Why we want to put on makeup to correct the dark circles under our eyes. And even circumstances unrelated to image prove this quandary to be true. The desire to correct or perfect the imperfectable is why we lie. To hide our fault or to hide our mistake. We *know* we should be better, but instead, we just cast blame on others. We take the spotlight that is revealing our imperfection off ourselves and shine it on someone else. But it is also why we get angry at injustice. Because we desire for all things to be made right, made fair, made just, and made new.

This desire, this bent, is a *good* bent. I believe it is *good* to recognize just how divine, with a restless *pursuit* of the divine, we have been made to be.

Where we begin to get in trouble is when we try to mask our inherent imperfectability and place expectations on ourselves (and others) to be and perform as such.

SPIRITUAL INJECTABLE

There was a time in my life when I was like a sugar-coated Peep dipped in honey, then slathered in birthday-cake icing and covered in rainbow sprinkles. Ew. Too sweet. No one's buying that.

I didn't want anyone to look at me and wonder whether or not I had a sincere relationship with God, so I tried to say and do the right thing at all times. I felt a constant need to prove to people that I was a "good" person. Embarrassingly, I, too, battled the inherent need to be a Christian outdoing others in their holier-than-thou Christiandom. Constantly pretending like I had it all together. Constantly defining myself by how my goodness and beauty were perceived.

Until the occasional time when I just couldn't keep up with my oh-so-perfect moral mentality. I would slip and falter and make an emergency appointment to get my dosage of twenty units of spiritual injectables.

Bibbidi Bobbidi Boo. Every sin corrected. Every natural bent toward immorality gone. Perfection achieved!

I walked around with perfectly taut desires, and flawless choices, and the purest of hearts. The best part? Everyone could see it! My spirituality was perfect and I wore it proudly…until the three to five months were up, that is.

In a nutshell, spiritual Botox is anything we use to maintain an *appearance* of goodness. We use different kinds of spiritual injectables to achieve the goal of apparent goodness, but it all comes in the form of self-righteousness.

Spiritual Botox is obsessed with the perception of spirituality or goodness, where there may not be much or any of it at all. The problem with perception is that it is not always real. And almost always, what we perceive is never the full story. We cannot ever rely on our goodness or *perception of* goodness and beauty to be our identity.

When *goodness* or apparent goodness becomes a goal or an identity to maintain, then we must ask the question, How good is good enough? How much goodness do I need to be sustainable? How good do I need to be to finally feel okay with myself? How good do I need to be around others so that they know me as good? And how much good must I do before God so that I am accepted by Him? What does being "good" even mean?

Is there really a metaphorical spiritual injectable that can fix the state of our humanity? Of course not. So, why are we so afraid to be real about our human nature?

PRETTY PRETEND

One Sunday morning, a pastor of a little church was invited into the children's Sunday school class to share a lesson. Once all the children were seated and quiet, the pastor began describing a squirrel to illustrate a point. "I am going to describe something and I want you to raise your hand when you know what it is." The children nodded eagerly.

He continued. "This thing lives in trees ... and it eats nuts ... and it has a long bushy tail ... " No hands went up. The pastor was surprised. He continued but to no avail. Not a hand was raised.

Finally, sensing the pastor's frustration, a little boy

named Billy raised his hand. The pastor breathed a sigh of relief and called on him. "Yes, Billy!"

The boy said, "Well, it sounds a lot like a squirrel to me...but I know the answer must be Jesus!"

The joke, while extraordinarily corny (and a little overused), is funny for one reason and one reason only: It's relatable. We've all been there and we've all seen it happen. Maybe to him, "Jesus" was the *perfect* answer, but squirrel was definitely the *right* answer. Because, ya know, sometimes Jesus is just not the answer.

"Who won the game yesterday?"

Jesus.

"What are you looking at on your phone?"

Jesus.

We laugh, but the truth is, it reflects how we all want to portray ourselves to others as more holy and righteous than we really are (and most often it comes off looking just as ridiculous). But when we do that, we forget something important. No matter how "good" we may appear, what truly counts is the condition of our heart. Because, even if we *say* "Jesus," do we really mean it?

No matter how hard we try to stake our flag at the top of Mount Perfection, at the end of the day, there will always be a big ol' boulder that stands in our way: sin.

Now, the real problem arises when we don't acknowledge the sin and work on it—slowly and prudently—and instead mask it with a few pixels of perfection and some bouts of spiritual Botox. *I mean, paper covers rock, right?* It may win in a game of rock, paper, scissors, but at the end of the day, the rock is still there. Because, when we try to cover it up, things get a little sticky.

I've got no problem with Photoshop or modern medicine. I do, however, have a problem when we stunt our spiritual growth. Because so often the actual thing being pursued is *not* goodness or moral perfection itself, but only the *appearance of it*. In other words, it's pride.

The reality? I sin, you sin, we all sin for more sin. When we want to pretend like we *don't* sin—like we are the chosen people of embodied righteousness walking around on a moral high ground—we begin to live a life of pretty pretend. It might look nice to others who may not know better, but it's ignoring the issues and masking the problems. It is a blatant avoidance of reality. It's trying to be perfect instead of trying to be whole.

Think about this. Matthew 5:48 (NIV) says, "Be perfect, therefore, as your heavenly Father is perfect." Our first instinct might be, *Oh, man, there it is. We are called to be perfect. Let's bust out the needles and get to work on this little soul of mine.*

But the Greek origin of the word "perfect" here is *telos*, meaning "to be whole." It also means having reached its end and completion.

How would it shift our entire approach to life, spiritual injections, self-righteousness, and the climb to the top of Mount Perfection if we were to read this passage as, "Be whole, therefore, as your heavenly father is whole"?

It makes it not about appearance but about our wholeness. Not as perfectible beings, but as *human* beings.

Flawed and lovely and on the not-so-fast track of redemption.

It makes us flip the script. It's not about, *How do I become perfect?* But instead, *How do I become fully and wholly human, metaphorical wrinkles and zits and all?*

Wholeness is a matter of harmony—body, soul, and spirit. It is living in such a way that all aspects of our lives are interconnected in a life-giving, intentional, and resilient way.

When we sin (and have an open heart to learn from said sin), God can use that to teach us of His perfection on behalf of our imperfection, so that we might be whole. Here's the funny thing about the word *telos*. The root (*tel-*) means "reaching the end (*aim*)." It helps to think of an old pirate's telescope—unfolding and extending one stage at a time to function at full strength. Bit by bit, the sections extend to reach full capacity and full function, and only then can the crusty old pirate see everything clearly.[2]

This little etymology lesson reveals that Matthew 5:48 is about how we were made to function. And guess what? We aren't even expected (or designed) to be perfect—the ultimate perfection is only in God Himself. Despite the fact that you and I are merely humans who are unable to fully "be good," God became man in the person of Jesus Christ to be fully human and fully perfect on my behalf and yours. Now, that is something I can identify with.

In that identity, I rest and live and *try* to be the best I can be. Like the telescope, I try to learn, bit by bit, to see everything clearly so that I, too, can live life in wholeness. I don't *try* in life because perfection is the goal but because perfection was already achieved by Someone actually *able* to achieve it. Don't try when it comes to perfection—*try* when it comes to your humanity. God is on a mission to make everyone a living telescope, to make us all understand who we were made to be. He will make *everything* new. He can and will redeem all things.

You were not mistakenly left here on Earth when God intended you for the perfection of heaven. You were not made to maintain a perception of morality. You were not made to be a false perception of perfection maintained by spiritual Botox that will fade. No, He does not make mistakes. You are perfectly intended, and your imperfections are what God uses to illuminate *His* perfection.

When the spotlight hits us and our imperfections are on display (yes, I'm talking about *you*, Velma the Volcano), we need not enter into existential-crisis mode about our security and worthiness as people, but instead we must turn the spotlight to God and *His* perfection. We are not held under the thumb of perfect expectation; we are expected to be perfectly imperfect human beings.

Remember, the goal is not perfection. The goal is *redemption*. This is our story. You are intended. You are loved. You are worthwhile. You are redemptive. Repeat.

THE TENSION

BEAUTY AWAKENING

The last sliver of golden light hangs on the horizon like the edge of a sheet of paper, getting thinner and thinner with each passing moment. Anticipation. You unknowingly hold your breath awaiting, drawing in the final rays of light until the sun sleepily dips below the earth, and the sky fades to black. The divine resolve.

Letting out a warm sigh, your eyelids slowly shut, and as they open back up, the sides of your mouth follow suit, turning heavenward in a soft smile. The end of the day and the beginning of the evening. Peace.

It seems that all of life can be like watching that last sliver of golden light. It is beautiful and pleasant, but we are left wanting the resolve. Much like if you stop a song before the final chord, it feels unfinished. We long for the resolve.

This is often the way I feel when I am traveling on the road and staying in a hotel. The hotel is perfectly grand and inviting—in fact, I have everything I need—but still, in no way does it feel like home.

Home is the place where your heart is at its resolve—there your heart can rest. And in my life, I have often found my heart to be the least contented and the most contented at the same time. Perfectly enjoying the beauty of the sunset, but simultaneously waiting for the finality of the setting. Similarly, I am content in my life here on Earth but feel the strong bent toward heaven and a pull to the divine.

I feel it in the soft sweetness of warm air after a summer rain, or in the sound of a match being lit as I listen to the snowfall outside. I hear it in the honking of a flock of geese as they head home for the winter in their carefully designed arrow. I feel it in the gentle beam of sunlight breaking through the clouds and trees while I drive with the windows down and a crisp breeze brushes my forearm. Each of these moments serves almost like a reminder of something fleeting, a memory, something I can't quite put my finger on.

Have you ever been struck by something that makes you want to go back to a place that you can't quite identify?

The moment is evanescent. And the minute it's gone is the moment when we long for its return. The Germans have a word for this: *sehnsucht*. At its simplest, it means "longing" or "yearning."

For C. S. Lewis, a permanent sense of *sehnsucht* characterized his deepest-held beliefs about Christianity. It was "that unnameable something, desire for which pierces us like a rapier at the smell of a bonfire, the sound of wild ducks flying overhead, the title of *The Well at the World's End*, the opening lines of *Kubla Khan*, the morning cobwebs in late summer, or the noise of falling waves."[1]

In *The Weight of Glory*, Lewis argues that we've all experienced this longing—and are embarrassed by it. *Sehnsucht* is "the secret also which pierces with such sweetness that when, in very intimate conversation, the mention of it becomes imminent, we grow awkward and affect to laugh at ourselves; the secret we cannot hide and cannot tell, though we desire to do both. We cannot tell it because it is a desire for something that has never actually appeared in our experience. We cannot hide it because our experience is constantly suggesting it, and we betray ourselves like lovers at the mention of a name."[2]

Another way of putting it? *Sehnsucht* is a feeling of nostalgia that faces toward the future. It's a home we've felt but never been to. It's a waiting for that sweet resolve that could lead to ultimate rest.

But like we talked about in the last chapter, though we long for that perfection, we aren't there yet. In fact, we will not be there until all of creation is redeemed—made perfect by God. This is the tension, the awaiting, the story of redemption we are living in now. We are restless souls with the image of our Creator painted into us, but we are not yet perfect representations. Humanity and Divinity. Earth and Heaven.

THE SCHOOL OF ATHENS

Earth is a planet in a galaxy of 100 billion stars. A globe suspended in the atmosphere, rotating and held together by forces we have come to be familiar with. But heaven? Heaven is unknown. Heaven is divine. Heaven is the paramount resolve where our hearts will be ultimately at rest forever.

I *long* for that rest. I long for not just a taste of the divine, but a feast. Not simply a poor reflection of divinity in a mirror, but the living embodiment of God Himself. I long not just to be (as worthy a calling as it is) a walking *Arnolfini Portrait*, but an actual perfect creation of God.

There is another famous painting that illustrates this dichotomy. In 1508, Raphael—one of the masters of the Italian Renaissance—was commissioned by Pope Julius II to paint several rooms in the Vatican. So, Raphael chose the theme of how classical Greece and Rome influenced Christianity in Italy through spiritual and worldly wisdom. The murals embody the classic origins of theology, law or literature, poetry or music, and philosophy. The last (and my personal favorite) of these is *The School of Athens*.

I'm sure you've seen it, and if you haven't, it's definitely worth a look. In it is a crowd of some of the greatest intellectuals up to that point—mathematicians, philosophers, and scientists from classical antiquity—gathered together sharing their ideas and learning from one another. These people had all lived at different times, but here they are gathered together under one stunningly beautiful roof (that must have been some party).

Right there in the middle of the painting, where our eyes naturally focus, are arguably the world's chief thinkers—Plato and Aristotle.[3]

Plato is pointing up at the heavens while Aristotle is gesturing with his whole hand downward at the earth. So, what's the topic of light conversation at this grand cocktail party? The place of human beings in the grand scheme of things. So simple. So easy.

Well, it has been said that the more things change the more they remain the same. Over 500 years later and we, too, still have one hand pointing upward and the other gesturing downward. We are constantly fighting an existential battle—heaven or earth. Beauty of what's to come versus the apparent reality of what is.

The best part of this painting? Well, just like our friend Jan van Eyck who painted the *Arnolfini Portrait*, Raphael painted himself right into the painting—and beautifully, he is the only one making direct eye contact with the viewer. Almost as if he gets the joke. That all the talk and all the debate and all the philosophizing still leads to the reality that no matter how high-minded our thoughts are, we are still called to live right here. Right now. As image bearers filled with our own unique identities, despite the tension existing in our hearts and all around us.

THE TENSION

We have a Bible study for the wives and girlfriends of players on our team that meets every couple weeks during the baseball season. After missing a night due to a hectic travel schedule, I ran into one of my favorite baseball wives of all time. She gave me a hug and we chatted a bit. When I asked her how Bible study was, she said, "It was good! But we missed you; you always bring a little bit more Jesus to the group."

I laughed loudly and said, "I'm definitely not anywhere close to that comparison. I feel a little more like I'm stuck somewhere between Jesus and 2Pac." She and I laughed as we grabbed our purses and headed to the game to watch our hubbies play.

A few days later, this same friend handed me a hot-pink gift bag. I reached inside and pulled out a gray two-tone T-shirt. As the shirt rolled out of its creased folds, it revealed 2Pac's giant face, smack-dab in the middle. I jumped up and down in overwhelming excitement and immediately made a wardrobe change. Later that night when I saw my husband, I pointed to the T-shirt and said, "This is me. Stuck somewhere between Jesus and 2Pac." He laughed, immediately getting the joke.

It was interesting to me that neither my friend nor my husband needed further explanation of my amusing comparison. I think this is because I believe we all feel this tension. We all feel this restless soul quandary that we must grapple with, sometimes on a daily basis—2Pac and Jesus. Divinely human and humanly divine.

This tension we live in reminds me of a tightrope walker. Have you ever seen a video of someone walking on a piece of cable attached to two opposite-facing buildings? It always sends involuntary shivers down my spine. The only thing that is allowing the person to walk between the two points (aside from skill and practice) is the cable itself. The cable must be properly taut and tied between the two points. Can you imagine someone throwing a slack rope between two thirty-story buildings and saying, "Hey, walk on this!"

No one would even attempt it.

But carefully tie a firm cable at the base of two trees (meaning, no more than six inches off the soft, grassy, padded ground) and I would totally try it! Why? Well, besides the fact that it lowers the risk of what would happen if I were to fall, physics is now on my side! The tension of the cable would allow me to attempt to walk on the tightrope!

Furthermore, did you know that tension is actually a *pulling* force? Think about the tension that is exerted by a rope when you pull something. Ropes cannot push anything; they are *meant* to pull. It may help to visualize a dog sled team. If the dogs were behind the sled attempting to push it with the ropes that were secured to them, they probably would not win any races. But with the ropes appropriately secured behind the dogs, they are able to go in front of the sled, using the force of the ropes to pull it.

What's the point and how on earth (pun intended) does this relate to us? You and I live in this tension between humanity and divinity. Between Earth and Heaven. And that very tension is meant to *pull* us closer to God!

Richard Baxter, an English Puritan, wrote *The Saints' Everlasting Rest* when he was facing a terminal illness, and he gave us the perfect response to this tension and feeling of longing:

> Why are not our hearts continually set on heaven? Why dwell we not there in constant contemplation? Bend thy soul to study eternity, busy thyself about the life to come, habituate thyself to such contemplations, and let not those thoughts be seldom and cursory, but bathe thyself in heaven's delights.
>
> A heavenly mind is a joyful mind; this is the nearest and truest way to live a life of comfort, and without this you must need be uncomfortable. Can a man be at a fire and not be warm; or in the sunshine and not have light? Can your heart be in heaven, and not have comfort? [On the other hand,] what could make such frozen, uncomfortable Christians but living so far as they do from heaven?...O Christian, get above. Believe it, that region is warmer than this below.[4]

This tension is not only a good tension, but it is also a *necessary* tension. It keeps us appropriately heavenly minded and reminds us that any desire for perfection is merely hinting at something to come. Rather than tether our identity to fickle, inappropriate expectations of earthly perfection, we must learn to tether our identity to our heavenly minded humanity!

I am what I am. We are who we are.

But who am I and who are you? We are creations of the Divine, who is perfection in and of Himself. Identifying in this tension—a heavenly minded humanity—keeps us like Plato, constantly pointing upward, while still understanding why Aristotle gestures to the earth. The result? Peace and confidence.

THE JOY OF MY REST

It was 2008, and I was sitting on the off-white carpet in the living room of our one-bedroom apartment somewhere in southern Florida, trying to finish a track for a new song. My keyboard was plugged into a blank white wall, and I was working endlessly on my next record while my husband was away at the field, playing Minor League baseball. Ben and I had been married for two years at the time, and we were slowly adjusting to life as husband and wife.

Because we made only $200 every two weeks and we had no credit card, I had to find some way to make a little extra cash for our newlywed bank. So I worked at the team store. I would stand behind the counter, helping people check out with their hats and T-shirts and blankets, all sporting the team name and sometimes even the gear showing my new last name. On this particular day,

I was nearly late leaving for the stadium because I was bound and determined to find the right kick for this track.

Clicking through hundreds of kick sounds in my recording program, I just couldn't land on the right one. With a sigh, I lay back on the carpet that had a residual smell from the previous renters. *What is that smell...curry? I love curry. I think I need a snack.*

The honest truth? I needed a great many things in that moment. I needed to find the right kick. I needed to leave for work. I needed more time in the day to finish my songs. Ben and I needed more money. And, yes, I needed a snack. Sensing my spiral into the Land of Whimpering, I placed my hands on my head and prayed. Out loud, I recounted the many gifts I had in my life: my health, my new husband whom I just so happen to be obsessed with, this keyboard that he gave me as a wedding gift, a passion for writing, a job, a crazy travel schedule that kept me very diligent with my time, and joy.

Joy. It flooded through me and around me like a warm, all-encompassing hug.

Oddly enough, it was especially in moments like these—moments of fear and lack and frustration—that I found immense and uncontainable joy, because I trusted that God had a plan for my life, that I was there for a reason, and that I am what I am. That identity that rested in a restless heavenly minded soul gave me *life* here. Joy. Identity. Humanity. Longing.

Overwhelmed by a feeling of joy and a lack of contentment at the same time, I sat up and grabbed my notebook.

Hastily taking my pen to paper, I scribbled down the words to a song. Words outpouring from the revelation of this obvious tension in my heart. The journey this revelation led me down was one of peace and resolve. The resolve that I could be confident in the fact that I was intended for Earth—I am what I am—but also the resolve that there is, at the same time, divine joy and peace to be found in the restless longing for Heaven.

If my life is dull
Pained with complaint and drought
Is it not my own fault
That I have shut the light out?
In my want of love to God
I need only to lift my heart
Take my mind to the Heavens
And stare at the one
How Great Thou art

The joy of my rest
Is delighted in nothing less
Than the taste of eternity
Heavenly mindedness
A lively soul
Hidden in the presence of a
Mighty Lord

Like candy in the mouth of a child
Is Heaven in the souls of saints

It would be a losing effort
To try and take it away

Yet so many have not tasted
So many have not even seen
Or heard the Heavenly song
That everyone can sing

The joy of my rest
Is delighted in nothing less
Than the taste of eternity
Heavenly mindedness
A lively soul
Hidden in the presence of a
Mighty Lord

How can we live confident and peaceful lives? We must first be at peace in our humanity. You are not more than human, and you are not less than human. Your identity is your humanity.

Confidence is found when we identify in the image of God—not our own imperfect image. We must understand that our longing for perfection is not a goal to try to accomplish, but a longing for God Himself. We must identify with the goodness of God, not with our poor attempts at spiritual Botox—perceived morality or goodness. We must find our identity in both our human and spiritual natures and be at peace that we were created for this tension. Created *by* God and *for* God.

We are part of a redemptive story, not a story of perfection. We are part of a confident story, not a story in which the characters are attempting to be someone other than themselves. We are part of a collaborative story, not a story of competition. We are part of a unified story, not a story of uniformity. We are part of a joyful story, not a story obsessed with quantifying or qualifying our relationship with God nor a story obsessed with quantifying and qualifying ourselves against one another.

The longing for the divine while living human lives is the pulling force of tension that will bring us closer to God, not to pride. Our bent toward heaven will not result in the feeble attempts of perfectionism but will result in a peace of mind that is content in being who we are: divine humans in faithful anticipation of the Divine Himself.

PART

SECURITY

THREE

10

THE UNINHIBITED LIFE

MATTE OR SHINY

Kruse and I went to lunch for a mommy–daughter date. After chicken tenders and salad topped off with a hot chocolate for her and coffee for me, we were walking down the main street in Roscoe Village when we came upon a nail salon. We didn't have an appointment booked, but it was a very modest-looking place, so we decided to be spontaneous and see if we could get our nails done. After informing the nail tech (who was already busy at work on someone else's calluses) that we wanted to get manicures, she told us to go pick out our color.

This *should* be the fun part.

Kruse hurried off in excitement, thrilled by the rows upon rows of colorful polishes that to me induced more anxiety. It was like being in a grocery store that has an entire aisle dedicated to sliced bread. Or being asked to fill out a living will. Or standing in front of thousands of Hallmark cards trying to pick out the perfect one for my mother-in-law.

For someone who hates to play favorites when it comes to color, I was anything but confident at that moment. Picking out a color sent me into a brain spin as I thought about what I had going on that week: *What color of nail polish will be good for what event? Maybe green—but what shade of green? Matte or shiny? But does this color even look good on my skin?! Screw it, I'm going with black. In subtractive color mixing, all the colors combined create black, so technically I'm not choosing a favorite. Plus, black goes with everything.*

"Okay, Mommy, I picked out my colors!" Kruse said, walking over to me holding three nail polish bottles in between her fingers and four more colors in the crook of her arm.

"Oh, wow! Let me help you, love," I said, trying not to reveal my panic that she might drop them all. I bent to help her hold the small bottles of every color of the rainbow she had picked out.

"One, two, three, four, five, six, seven!" I counted aloud, hoping she wouldn't sense how humorous I found this. "You chose seven colors!"

Not ten colors, not five, not one, but seven. Ignoring all laws of arithmetic and color coordination, she proudly held a deep red, an orange, a mustard yellow, a green, a pink, a hot pink with sparkles, and a vibrant purple. She was basically holding an off-beat ROYGBIV in her hands. I loved it.

We sat down next to each other. The nail technicians made small talk with each other while Kruse and I chatted about other things. Suddenly I could see in her eyes that she wanted to say something.

"You okay?" I asked.

"Uh, I actually wanted the yellow on this finger," she whispered to me, pointing at the ring finger of her left hand.

"Okay, can you just ask the lady politely if she will switch it?"

"Excuse me, can you please put yellow on this finger instead?" she asked in such a way it felt as if there were sugared rainbow pieces being sprinkled all over the room (call me biased).

The nail technician responded graciously, dipping a cotton ball on the top of the nail polish remover and gently removing yellow from Kruse's thumb, and then painting the yellow on her ring finger.

A few minutes and a few fingers later, Kruse spoke up again. "Um, excuse me. Will you please put the purple on my pinkie?" More sugary rainbow bits fell over the room with her very words.

This time I could sense the nail technician's growing annoyance. She looked over at me with a look that said more than words could have. The "uh-are-you-going-to-say-something" look. My immediate knee-jerk reaction was to respond with, "Oh, Kruse, it's fine, honey. Let's be grateful."

But thankfully, before saying that, I immediately realized what sloppy thinking that is! To desire for your nails
to be painted a certain way doesn't make you *un*grateful.
In fact, Kruse was so obviously appreciative and enjoying
every minute of this special occasion. She simply had a
vision in her imagination, an idea that would express her
own unique self-expression and creativity! So, I was faced
with a decision... Respond to please the nail tech and
shut down Kruse's creativity in the name of "gratitude," or
respond in a way that would champion Kruse and validate
her creative imagination.

"I think she chose such fun colors, don't you?" I said to
the nail tech, nodding toward Kruse with a smile. I tried
to muster as much sweetness as I could, but alas, there
were no figurative sugary rainbow bits falling from the
heavens when I spoke. I could feel the nail technician's
annoyance with me, but she said nothing as she painted
Kruse's pinkie the vibrant purple.

A little while later our manicures were complete and
Kruse skipped out of the salon, thanking me again and
again, blissfully unaware of the nail tech's abrupt change
in attitude. My little girlie was so excited for the wild array
of color on her fingers, and I felt like I had been handed
an incredibly important life lesson.

That mommy–daughter date had me thinking long and
hard about the difference between Kruse and me when it
came to the process of choosing colors. She *knew* what
she loved, she did *not* ask my opinion, she could not
have cared *less* whether a color looked good on her skin,

and she did not *apologize* for knowing the vision she saw in her imagination and for asking it to be carried out in that way. I learned that day that colors don't need to make sense to anyone else if they make sense to *you*. I learned that there is something vulnerable and truly *self*-expressive when we do not seek affirmation (the "Yes, that looks great with your skin tone!" or "Yes, I love that color!" approval) from others when it comes to creative expression. I learned that creativity takes guts. I learned that we are all artistic geniuses. The somber realization I came to that day is that many of us grow out of touch with our imagination, creative expression, and artistic loves.

PETER PAN AND HAIRBALLS

I would love to see Peter Pan take an art class.

I can imagine the little mischief-maker dressed in his typical green garb listening to his art teacher (but only close enough to get the basic idea) and then taking complete creative liberty on the canvas. Head down. Never looking around or glancing about at other students' work. Completely and wholeheartedly invested in what is in front of him. *Oh, I'll just draw this giant pirate ship that can magically float through the air while a tick-tocking crocodile follows close behind.*

What is it about children that allows them to be so fearlessly creative and expressive? At what point do we take our eyes off our own canvas and start glancing around 'at others'? At what point do we begin to measure our own self-expression against others'?

It seems that children flourish where adults fail. Children are more creative and are naturally inclined to invent. Their worldview is incomplete and demands discovery. They embrace their own ignorance instead of ignoring it. They are willing to explore, investigate, and put their ideas to the test because failure is futile. Unlike adults, they don't care what people think of their ideas, and they have little to no concern with reality.

But, sure, growing up can have its benefits. Our brainpower sharpens and our willpower strengthens. We set goals and hone skills. But there is a price to pay with all this growing up—we lose our precious naiveté that enables creativity. Picasso was right when he said, "Every child is an artist. The problem is how to remain an artist once we grow up."

And at what point do we begin to believe *I am not an artist*?

Well, as it turns out, a study was conducted by Darya Zabelina and Michael Robinson of North Dakota State University to explore just that. Some psychologists divided a large group of undergraduates into two groups. The first group was given the following prompt: You are seven years old. School is canceled, and you have the entire day to yourself. What would you do? Where would you go? Who would you see?

The second group was given the same prompt minus the first sentence. Rather than imagining themselves as seven years old, they approached the question with their own adult mind-set.

Next, the psychologists asked their subjects to take ten minutes to write a response. Afterward, the subjects were given various tests of creativity, such as inventing alternative uses for an old tire or completing incomplete sketches. Zabelina and Robinson found that "individuals [in] the mindset condition involving childlike thinking . . . exhibited higher levels of creative originality than did those in the control condition."[1]

The proof is in the pudding.

Gordon MacKenzie, a card maker at Hallmark for thirty years, wrote a brilliant and inspiring book called **Orbiting the Giant Hairball**. It has been in my top five favorite books for a while now. There is one part that really stuck with me. It describes when he visited schools to teach welding to children:

"Hi! My name is Gordon MacKenzie, and among other things, I am an artist. I'll bet there are artists here, too . . . How many artists are there in the room? Would you please raise your hands?"

The pattern of responses never varied.

First Grade:

En mass the children leapt from their chairs, arms waving wildly, eager hands trying to reach the ceiling. Every child was an artist.

Second Grade:

About half the kids raised their hands, shoulder high, no higher. The raised hands were still.

Third Grade:

At best, 10 kids out of 30 would raise a hand. Tentatively. Self-consciously.

And so on up through the grades. The higher the grade, the fewer children raised their hands. By the time I reached sixth grade, no more than one or two did so...[2]

If you and I had been sitting cross-legged next to one another in that class in first grade, we would have wildly raised our hands and unapologetically agreed that we are artistic and creative. You and I would have been filled with full confidence in our own individual artistry. But as we learn to compare, we learn the devastating art of disregarding our creativity because it does not measure up to what so-and-so is doing. The killer of creativity is this: devaluing our intrinsic self-expression and play.

So, how do we learn to play again? How do we shake the feelings of insecurity and fear of perception in order to imagine and express ourselves in meaningful ways?

Here are ten simple things that yours truly does to dig up that magical childlike lack of inhibition:

1. Try enjoying the rain and dancing in it the way a child does.

2. Buy a disco ball and turn it on for breakfasts in the morning with the kiddos. If you get the battery-operated kind, turn it on in the car for a girls' night. Basically, disco balls just make life better.

3. There is something about having to climb over two rows of seats in the car and being able to look out a back window that just gives me a different perspective on life. Any time we can offer ourselves a unique perspective on life, it will spark new thoughts and imagination and creativity. Plus, it'll keep ya limber.

4. Team up with a bestie or with your mom or spouse, and every other month send each other an art medium to experiment with. You can start off easy with something like canvas, and give yourself a couple weeks to finish. As you experiment with different art forms, you will have to begin to get more creative. Use foam and see what you can create, or try clay and see what you sculpt. The more you do this, the easier it will get!

5. The next time you sit down at your piano or keyboard or guitar to write a song, break the rules. Don't focus on two verses, a bridge, and a chorus; just write.

6. Why do kids love paper airplanes so much? Duh, because they're fun. Go make one.

7. Around the dinner table we like to ask our children bizarre unrealistic questions to spark imagination—and of course answer them ourselves too. If you could have one superhuman power, what would it be and why? If you had to wear only one color for the rest of your life, which color would you choose and why? If you could have a house made out of anything, what would you have and why? (By the way, mine would totally be gummy bears.)

8. As we grow into adulthood, we grow in confidence of our opinions. However, what I observe in myself sometimes is that I might grow in confidence, but I grow away from my confidence to answer the question, "Why? Why am I so convinced of this opinion I have?" If you ask a child why they think or believe something, rarely (and never in the case of my own kids) do I hear the reply "I don't know." Why is that? Because they are in the process of *learning*. The reasoning behind their replies is never far behind.

9. *Never* stop learning. Perhaps you have the time to take an online class. Perhaps you only have time for a monthly book club with the other neighborhood stay-at-home moms and dads. Maybe you have always wanted to take a cooking class or a dance class or a fencing class. Whatever you do, just continue to learn new things.

10. Practice the art of intrinsic response. Collect art

simply because it makes you feel something, not because it matches your house. Open up your creative mind to connect with like-minded creatives. I've always said I would rather have an empty wall than a meaningless wall. Do not buy art (from Target or HomeGoods or the most expensive gallery in NYC) just to fill space. Allow yourself the enjoyment of happening upon art that makes you feel something...wonder, contentment, glumness, uncertainty, or puzzlement.

The most childlike woman I've ever known is my eighty-five-year-old aunt Marilyn. Child*ish* she most certainly is not. Gracing a full spread in *Fortune* magazine back in the 1970s for her business savvy and prowess as a female, Aunt Marilyn has discovered the importance of maintaining her childlike intuition. She comically refers to herself as the Energizer Bunny, bending her knees to brace herself for a full-on hug from my sprinting children. She never apologizes for things she does not need to apologize for (she orders her hash browns "extra crispy" and will smile graciously and ask for them to be sent back if they are not cooked to her liking). Walking into Aunt Marilyn's home is like walking into a life-sized pop-up book full of her memories and travels. Every knickknack has a story, and every piece of art brings stars to her eyes as she recounts the memories she and her late husband made through their lives together. Despite battling cancer, Aunt Marilyn continues to send birthday gifts to each of my children and is always up for a shopping trip when she and I are together. She knows what she loves, much like my little Kruse in the nail salon, and does not apologize for it. She offers to jump in the back seat whenever we pick her up for brunch. When I asked her what she believes has helped her maintain her childlike lack of inhibition, she giggled and said, "I eat breakfast standing up. In fact, rarely do I sit down."

REWIND

There is a girl in my house who moves effortlessly through the world.

It is not that everything comes easily for her. She gets frustrated at a lot of little things. She drops her doll in the movie theater and begins to cry. She suddenly breaks out in tears at the littlest inconveniences. She works hard on her homework and sometimes struggles with her science assignments, but she moves through the day with a certain amount of effortlessness and whimsy—unbound and uninhibited.

I will watch her, mesmerized, as she breaks out into twirls and wiggly, giggly dances. She is a girl who travels in cartwheels, making her way to the bowl of cherry tomatoes, spinning and spinning, just for a handful, only to turn around and spin some more, just because she thought it would be a fun form of transportation.

Sometimes she will make her way through the living

room as a robot, rigid arms moving up and down and then suddenly dropping them to dangle at a right angle. Sometimes a zombie, with a glazed look in her eyes. Sometimes a ballerina, who glides through the room without care. Sometimes she's a rhino, giant feet stomping down the wooden steps.

Beyond selections in nail polish, there is so much I can learn from this girl. There is no outward attempt at being "different" and there is no fight to be the same. She just makes decisions based on what she wants to do, and sometimes, yes, it makes absolutely no sense. She moves through her world being who she is, and it doesn't matter what people are thinking of her... at least not yet.

Once we become aware of ourselves, we can't forget ourselves. What my little girlfriend has taught me is that we must, instead, embrace who we are. We must move more like children—unbound, uninhibited, and unapologetic about our weird and quirky inclinations. We've got to remember that our very weirdness is what makes this world hilarious, interesting, and beautiful. We've got to express the very selves that we've become far too aware of.

Psychologically, inhibition means a restraint on the direct expression of an instinct. It's fear. It's insecurity. It's second-guessing why we make the natural choices we make. So, to combat that feeling is to enforce creative self-expression, or simply express yourself in some form. Whether it be through art, music, fashion, or writing, it all comes down to *just being yourself*. It's also what people refer to as that *state of flow*—that timeless state you're in where you are not really aware of what you're doing.

To borrow from Pablo Picasso again, he paints a perfect picture (no pun intended) of what uninhibited self-expression looks like in practice:

> I don't know in advance what I am going to put on canvas, any more than I decide beforehand what colors I am going to use. While I am working, I am not conscious of what I am putting on the canvas. Each time I undertake to paint a picture, I have a sensation of leaping into space. I never know whether I shall fall on my feet. It is only later that I begin to estimate more exactly the effect of my work.[3]

When he talks about not being conscious of what he is putting on the canvas, it's like his ego is getting out of the way. It's removing all sense of concern for what others might think or how it will be perceived once it's finished. It's taking himself out of the picture (ironically, by putting himself into the picture). But despite all the inhibition, there is one thing providing some limitations for the king of cubism: a canvas. Four corners. Four sides. With all the self-expression and breaking of rules, and playfulness, he still gave himself some parameters.

Much like children who naturally experience this state, *everything* is a form of self-expression. They're just being who they are. They don't think about the task itself or the end result; they just enjoy the moment.

MONKEY BARS AND FENCES

It's amazing how a simple slide can be the door to a mighty fortress. A swing can be a rocket ship to the sky. A merry-go-round can be a time machine. Monkey bars become the Amazon. And the floor? Lava, obviously.

But one feature of the playground that often goes unnoticed is the structure that surrounds it.

Child psychologists have done extensive studies on the necessity of fences when it comes to school playgrounds. In a nutshell, researchers wanted to see whether the visual awareness of a fence around the playground would increase creative play among the students or whether it would inhibit it.

Teachers took their children to a local playground where there was no fence. The kids were to play as normal. The same group was then taken to a comparable playground in which there was a fence.

In the first scenario, the children huddled around their teacher, fearful of leaving her sight. The second scenario exhibited drastically different results, with the children feeling free to explore within the given boundaries.

The overwhelming conclusion was that with a given limitation, children felt safer to explore a playground. Without a fence, the children were not able to see a given boundary or limit and thus were more reluctant to leave the teacher. There was no protection. An out-of-control vehicle could barrel through. A gang of thugs could freely enter the field. A stray dog could threaten the helpless children. But *with* a boundary, in this case the fence, the children felt at ease to explore. They were able to separate from the teacher and continue to develop their sense of self while still recognizing that they were in a safe environment.[4]

Turns out, much like Picasso's canvas, the physical fence provides much-needed parameters for creativity. We need to first be limited in order to become limitless.

So, what is the symbolic fence protecting our mental playground? What is the thing that will make us feel safe enough to play, create, and express?

The sense of security.

When you go on a roller coaster, workers walk up and down the sides of the car in order to ensure your belt is secure. When we secure something, we make it safe. When the workers pull down the barred constraint, it immediately offers a sense of safety, allowing you the peace of mind to really enjoy the ride.

If creativity is a roller coaster (applicable on so many levels), then the confines of creativity are really what allow us to feel secure enough to be. When I write songs with other writers, we call it being in the "safe room." This means that the room is safe, secure. It means that no idea is bad, so feel free to throw out your next idea concerning lyric or melody. Creating within the walls of a "safe room" is like the restraint on the ride that allows us to know the safe outcome, so we can enjoy the ride. Just as Picasso gave himself the four corners of the canvas and just as children need a visible fence in order to explore and imagine and *play*, so have we been given these four corners of a canvas, a fence, and a seat belt.

It might not be something physical that we can see and touch, but it is an ultimate, intrinsic belief of security in God. God made you the way He intended. He gave you a creative mind and made you a childlike genius with the ability to invent and daydream and imagine and create. You can feel secure and be secure within the confines or boundaries He has set in place!

The fence, in a spiritual sense, is the Word of God. He has done and said so much to give us assurance and security:

- "I have written this to you who believe in the name of the Son of God, so *that you may know* you have eternal life." (1 John 5:13 NLT)
- "*We know* that if the earthly tent we live in is destroyed, we have a building from God, a house not made with hands, eternal in the heavens...He who has prepared us for this very thing is God, who has given us the Spirit as a guarantee." (2 Corinthians 5:1–5 NIV)
- "Let us draw near with a true heart in *full assurance of faith*...Let us hold fast the confession of our *hope without wavering*." (Hebrews 10:21, 23 ESV)

God has seen fit to give us these specific moments in Scripture that act as our fence. I have so much room to play in life and to create with my imagination, because I know exactly where the fence is. We are encouraged to enjoy life and create and imagine and dream big and invent and run and jump and dress weird because He *made* us this way! If God's commandments and security in Scripture can act as our visible fence, and if His Word acts like a roller-coaster seat belt, then why wouldn't we enjoy playing on the open field? We aren't meant to fixate on the fence and the seat belt; we're meant to enjoy the ride—nail salons, playgrounds, roller coasters, and all.

11

THE COLOR KIDS

BLINDING COLORS

I was out in LA recording my first full-length record, *Shatterproof*. It had been a full week of writing and producing and singing the same line over a hundred times, but finally we were done! We had just wrapped up the last song and I was leaving the studio. With a few hours to kill before I had to fly out later that evening, I decided to take my suitcase in the car with me and head down to Melrose for a little alone-time celebratory shopping.

But first, food.

If you've forgotten, I was raised on organic garden-grown food *long* before it was trendy, and I know I've made my point that even as a healthy eater myself, I am very unimpressed with the License to Gasconade, awarded by "the cool" to those who eat clean.

At any rate, there was a restaurant on Melrose I had been to once before called Urth Caffé. I walked in wearing a tea-length bright- and light-blue-striped skirt. It was a skirt that originally had a sequined top attached to it as a bridesmaid dress, but one week and a few bucks at the alterations shop later, I had a quirky, full-volume, drapey-looking skirt. I styled it with multicolored high-top sneakers and a tucked-in white burn-out graphic Blondie T-shirt. Basically, Rainbow Brite and the Color Kids, circa 2015.

I waited in line until I was able to order my sandwich and drink. I ordered bubble tea simply because it sounded amusing and playful, then sat down at a small table for two. My structured hot-pink shoulder bag with gold metal lips on the front sat in the second chair. A waiter brought my order to me. As I began sipping my tea, I felt what seemed like tasteless fish eggs in my mouth—basically pudding balls. I resisted the urge to spit them out and tried to act cool about it. I looked up to see if anyone else was having the same reaction, but no, just Rainbow Brite over here.

However, during my second look around the restaurant, I realized it was hard to tell *what* others' reactions were. Why? Because almost every single person in that restaurant still had their sunglasses on. I glanced up to double-check that we were, indeed, inside a building with a roof. Yes, we were.

The cool factor was just simply too much to bear. The longer I looked around, the more I saw. Black on black on black on black on black on leather on black. These were monochromatic-sunglass-wearing kale eaters. *Holy cow, what am I doing here?! Maybe that's why they're wearing sunglasses—the light is reflecting off the colors I'm wearing in a way they have never seen!* I felt equally annoyed at them and embarrassed for myself. Here I was, a walking box of Crayola crayons, unaware of what bubble tea was . . . what an idiot!

The thoughts in my head frustrated me. *Why do I care that I clearly don't look like I'm from here? Why do I want to fit in so badly? Furthermore, do I even want to fit into the monochromatic-sunglass-wearing-kale-eating club?* Something had to be done.

Finishing my sandwich in a flutter and pitching the tea, I whizzed to my car. Popping the trunk open, I rummaged through my bag like a haphazard prospector to find my black leather pants and black boots.

Dang it! I don't have a black shirt. I sighed out loud. *Oh wait! Yes, I do. My pajama top! Brilliant.*

Slamming the trunk closed, I opened the door to the back seat and jumped in like a woman on a quest. As embarrassing as it is to admit, I did it. I changed in the back seat. I was going to deliberately try to fit in.

Stepping out of the car, I flipped my platinum hair to give extra rock-and-roll flair to the whole scene. Black boots, black leather pants, black bra, black slinky pajama tank, and . . . *green*-rimmed sunglasses. *Oh well.* I told myself, *Jules, you are going to go into Marc Jacobs wearing your sunglasses and I forbid you to take them off.*

I walked across the street faking confidence and trying to pump myself up to just try to attempt to look like I fit in. *Just keep those sunglasses on the entire time. Head down. Open the door. Don't make eye contact.* I stopped myself from rushing over to the neon plaid dress I saw over in the right corner of the brightly lit and merrily decorated store. Slowly turning on my heels, I made my way over to the rack with a lot of, well, black. As I pretended to shop, feeling more and more ridiculous as the seconds passed by, a twentysomething sales kid came up on my right.

"Can I help you find anything today?" he asked.

"Nah, I'm good," I said without looking up.

Head down, Jules, head down.

"Okay, well just let me know!" he responded kindly. "You must be a musician, huh?"

This is what we call immediate gratification. *Why, yes, yes, in fact, I am a very cool black-on-black-on-black-monochromatic-sunglass-wearing-kale-eating musician,* I thought.

"Yep!" I said with way too much cheer. *Play it cool, Jules, play it cool.*

"Right on. What type of music do you play?"

There it was. The unavoidable question. I resisted the urge to slowly and sheepishly pull my sunglasses off my nose.

"Uhhhh, Christian pop."

Now you're just a jerk, Jules, I thought to myself. *You're calling yourself a Christian and you haven't even been kind enough to look this kid in the eye yet. You're bogus and you know it!* Suddenly, the tiny animated Rainbow Brite herself popped up on my right shoulder and began ruthlessly (but justifiably) reprimanding this alter ego I had created. I couldn't take it any longer. I ripped my sunglasses off, looked him in the eye, and smiled. "I'm a Christian pop artist," I said again, this time with a confidence that I felt, a confidence that I owned.

"Oh, that's dope. I haven't been to church since moving here four months ago," he replied. "In fact, I haven't really met a Christian since moving here."

"Well, it's nice to meet you!" I said with a laugh, and shook his hand. Suddenly I felt like myself again. And in no time we were talking fashion and life and friends and career goals. I eventually made my way over to the neon plaid dress. So me. I bought the dress in blue, gave the kid a hug, and encouraged him to never quit on his goals.

I learned something about myself that day. I learned that to try to be anyone else is exhausting. I learned that God didn't make a mistake. He made me *me* so that I could achieve the things and the purpose that He has for *my* life. I learned that if I tried to become someone I was not, I could miss out on opportunities. And I learned that I'm not the black-on-black-monochromatic-sunglass-wearing-kale-eating girl I was trying to be. I'm a little more like Rainbow Brite.

If you *are* a monochromatic-kale-eating person, then be that. But just don't try to become someone you are not and certainly don't let the culture you are in, the city you are in, the church you are in, the community you are in, dictate *what* you look like and *how* you express yourself on the outside. Because as much as your self-expression might be met with resistance or misunderstanding, and as much as it feels like it would be easier to try to fit in, the world needs *you*. Not a false version of you.

SUBWAY OR CONCERT HALL

It was 7:51 in the morning of January 12, 2007. A scruffy dude in a Washington Nationals baseball cap made his way near the Washington, D.C., L'Enfant Plaza metro stop with nothing but his violin. He propped open his case on the ground, threw in a few coins as seed money, and started to play. He played some Bach, a Massenet, one Schubert, one Ponce for about forty-five minutes. It was rush hour, so about a thousand people passed him.

A middle-aged man noticed the musician. He slowed his pace and stopped to listen for only a moment before realizing that he had to make his way to work. After a few minutes the violinist received his first dollar.

One of the people who paid the most attention was a three-year-old boy. His mother pulled on his arm, but the kid fought to listen. Finally, the mother came from behind and pushed the boy so that he would continue to walk, but his head was still facing the musician. This happened a few times with other children, but the parents continued to force them to get up and go already.

In the forty-five minutes that the violinist gently stroked the strings with his bow, only six people stopped to listen. About twenty gave him a couple bucks but didn't stop to enjoy the music. This earned him a whopping thirty-two bucks. Not too bad. Seems about average for your everyday street performer.

But this random street performer was Joshua Bell, who is one of *the* best violinists in the world. That January morning, he played some of the most intricate pieces ever written on a violin worth $3.5 million. Turns out, only a couple of nights before that subway performance, he had played Boston Symphony Hall, and you can bet he made a lot more than thirty-two bucks, given that the average seat was a hundred dollars.[1]

The question begging to be asked is: Why didn't people recognize his music as great art when Bell was playing in the subway? Why didn't people stop to listen and enjoy the performance if it sounded the very same in the Boston Symphony Hall (and trust me, the acoustics ain't too bad in a subway stop)?

This particular day in the life of Joshua Bell tells us a lot about personal preferences and self-expression. Our proclivity toward our own choices in things like music, art, and fashion is not merely based on what we see or what we hear or what we feel. Rather, it's based on what we **believe** that thing to be.

This is why someone listening to the music of Joshua Bell is going to hear it differently and like it more if they believe it's from Joshua Bell. If you hear the same pieces by Johann Sebastian Bach from just an old, scruffy, unimportant street performer, it obviously doesn't sound as good.

It's why we prescribe certain value to paintings if they have an important signature in the corner. It's why an antique coming from a curated auction house has more value than it would if we just happened to see it in a Goodwill somewhere. It's why we think wine doesn't taste as good if you don't know it's an expensive wine from the valleys of southern France.

There *must* be a way to like something purely because we simply like it and not because culture, or New York Fashion Week, or a music critic, or sommeliers, or the city of Los Angeles tells us it is something we should like. Surely, personal preferences can be personal self-expression, which can come from the self...right?

Self-expression is a widely used phrase, but oddly enough it seems that whatever we're calling self-expression is not *self*-expression. Instead, it's more like an I-made-sure-this-creativity-was-approved-and-affirmed-by-one-or-maybe-two-other-people-before-owning-it type of expression. Which, by this time, is not an expression of simply *your*self, but an odd mixture of yours and a few other people's. When was the last time you went shopping with a friend and did *not* ask your friend's opinion on the dress that you already knew you loved? The key is to not be so burdened with what is "right" that we sacrifice what is expressive.

Holding on to your intrinsic self-expression means

never losing touch with what you love. It is to determine to never lose sight of your own self, your own natural proclivity toward certain preferences. Why does someone love roses over daisies? Why do I prefer the color green over the color yellow? Who knows! But cultural norms can get conflated with our own personal preferences, and forgetting our own natural tendency is easy to do.

YOUR INTERIOR DESIGN

Right now, I am sitting on a deep-set sofa in light gray, accessorized by pillows that have been stuck with pins of various images from an array of interests. My feet are propped on a seven-foot-by-seven-foot black-and-white checkered coffee table that basically doubles as a stage on an average Saturday morning here. On top of the black-and-white checkers are three massive M&M sculptures—red, orange, yellow. The coffee table sits on top of a multi-colored hot pink, orange, yellow, and turquoise rug, which lays upon a geometric-patterned area rug. In the corner is a three-foot-tall metal teddy bear. Mr. Teddy used to be a mold for creating teddy bears in Asia but now stands up-right looking like a pathetic protector of the northwestern corner of my house. There is a painting of several red-and-white peppermints, gummy bears, and gumballs on one wall. On another wall hangs an orange Fox with blue socks, and a yellow Sneetch with a green star on his belly.

Why am I telling you all of this? Because it's the visual

representation of what is in my heart. I wish you could each come visit and see the literal Candy Land explosion that is the Zobrist home. Perhaps it doesn't follow what they teach in interior design school. There may not be an allegiance to tried-and-true principles like color theory or balance, but each of these mismatched items and border-line bizarre design choices is a visual representation of a story from my life—a visual representation of *my* interior design.

The Dr. Seuss paintings of the Fox and the Sneetch could easily look like simple childhood storybook illus-trations, but in actuality, Dr. Seuss's art and writings are incredibly kindred to my somewhat subversive nature. *The Sneetches* particularly holds a very important place in my heart.

The Sneetches is about two types of creatures, sepa-rated by those who have stars on their bellies and those who do not. The Star-Belly Sneetches think they are the best and look down upon Sneetches without stars. The Plain-Belly Sneetches remain depressed and oppressed, prohibited from associating with their star-bellied coun-terparts, until Sylvester McMonkey McBean comes along with his Star-on and Star-off machines. He begins to give stars to the Plain-Belly Sneetches, and soon they are happy, because now they look like their elite star-bellied counterparts. The original Star-Belly Sneetches are an-gered, because now they no longer look different and special, so they get Sylvester to remove all their stars. This continues back and forth until no one can remember which Sneetches were originally what, and an epiphany strikes them all at once: It really doesn't matter whether a Sneetch has a star belly or not; they are all really the same. A Sneetch is a Sneetch.[2]

As you can imagine, the song of embracing and celebrating diversity of thought and appearance has always been a resounding drumbeat in my life.

The plain deep-seated sofa reveals that I value the snuggles and comfort of a comfortable living room. I want people to be able to sit and stay for a while. I want them to relax and talk and nap and cozy up with their loved one.

The M&M's are simply humorous, exorbitant in their extreme size. However, to me, I don't only see caricature-style candy. Instead, I remember the day I walked into a gallery in Phoenix with Zion. He ran to the sculptured M&M's, examined them closely, touched one ever so slightly, then turned to me and whispered with resolution, "Life needs candy."

The metal teddy bear in the corner reminds me that behind every soft cuddly bedtime teddy bear, there once was a metal frame, stoic and cold.

The faux fur chairs with vintage frames in front of the fireplace might look sophisticated and expensive to the eye, but to me they mean that I value quality and functionality. The old things that can withstand decades are now covered in a textile that is able to withstand chewed-up granola bars and spilled milk.

Self-expression is a way to communicate your inner world, which is why outward self-expression is a beautiful blend of both the internal and the external. In fact, I would argue that self-expression is 85 percent internal development and maybe only 15 percent external. All of these external things (the fur, the checkers, the colors, the obnoxious candy sculptures) are not really about the *things*—they are ultimately about the interior design of the designer. The interior design of me.

PICK YOUR FLAVOR

Say you're the girl who likes to wear drop-crotch sweatpants with sneakers, a tank, and a hoodie. You might be a chill girl—a girl who appreciates comfort, androgyny, or sports.

Say you're the girl who likes to wear tailored blazers and pleated pantsuits. You might be the girl who is always on time (super jealous of you) and will get your tasks done efficiently and effectively.

Say you're the girl with dreads and a loose-hanging dress over a loose pair of denim. You might be the girl who values ease and not having to spend time on getting ready. You might be the girl who doesn't wear tight jeans, not because you wouldn't look sexy in them, but because there is a political view you hold behind what you wear.

Say you're the girl with an eccentric mix of patterns and colors. Like me, you might be the girl who likes to mix things up. The girl who looks for the rules so she can break them.

The point is, self-expression—whether it's through interior design, personal style, music, art, or writing—communicates things about who you are. The result of your self-expression directly reflects what is going on on the inside.

When I talk to women about self-expression, the problem is not that they don't know *how* to freely express themselves, but rather that they have simply forgotten what it is they love. If you're reading this and thinking, *That is so me—after kids (or my promotion or taking on this new job or after moving to a new city) I just lost touch with myself!* then you would not be alone. Losing touch with what you love is easy to do! So, I want to take some time to talk about how we can get back in touch with that old friend: self-expression. For some of you, your creative expression manifests in the way you design your outfits or home. For others, this tapping back into a creative mind-set looks more like tapping back into music or writing. You are going to have to answer that question for yourself, but we are going to explore some creative practices to rediscover your natural proclivity.

Since one of my favorite mediums for self-expression is the way I dress, I am going to share with you some behind-the-scenes tidbits that have helped me in this area. Often when women ask me what my unique style is, I just simply say, "It's me! Anything I love!" If you want some help in discovering what it is that you actually *love*, I have a few instructions:

1. Buy a fashion magazine. Sit down on the floor with a cup of coffee during whatever time of day is inspiring to you, and without overthinking, mark the complete outfits you like. Circle them with a Sharpie or bend the corner of the page, but flip through quickly and mark every full look that you love. This shouldn't take you very long. We want you to begin tapping back into your "Oh my gosh, I love this!" response that has been on hiatus for a while. Don't look at the model's face; just look at the looks themselves, circle what you love, and turn the page. Easy-peasy. Don't force yourself to circle something if you do not get an immediate reaction from it. Now, go back through the magazine more slowly. The goal here is to begin connecting the similarities between the looks. *Weird. I always love the outfits that have layers upon layers.* Or *I'm always drawn to dresses with clean lines!* Or *I have circled literally every photo that has an all-black ensemble.* The goal of this exercise is not to pick out individual pieces that you can't live without. In fact, sometimes focusing too much on individual pieces can be confusing and you might end up wasting money on something that you won't be able to wear a lot. The goal for this exercise is to figure out your own unique style. Your own unique point of view—your natural proclivity!

2. Next, I'm going to ask you to do something bold. Go shopping *alone*. And I don't mean online. I want you to go to a mall of your choice and walk around with your phone to window-shop. Take photos of the mannequins whose outfits you have a natural and immediate response to. This exercise is about learning how to find things you like without having to rely on a bestie being with you to convince you to buy something that you may or may not actually like. Sometimes we need to give ourselves a little time and a little space and a little freedom from other opinions to really figure out what it is that we ourselves are moved by.

3. Set a budget for one outfit and go find it. I'm not saying rummage through racks and racks until you find one jacket that you'll get home and have no idea how to coordinate with the rest of your closet. I mean, print out one of the pics of the mannequins or tear out a photo of one of the outfits that you loved from the magazine and go find your own priced version of it from top to bottom. Maybe the outfit you loved was ankle-cropped black denim and a ripped-up band T-shirt and a colorful structured blazer. Head to wherever your budget allows and look for that outfit.

4. Now go out and rock your entire look with *confidence*, knowing that you can indeed pull it

off, not because your friend said she loved it and it looked great on you but because you singularly love it.

A commitment to expressing your true self and preferences is important because it is the way in which you express an attribute of God Himself. The way you dress, the way you do your hair, your nail polish color, the music you create, your imagination, your art, your research, your writing—all are reflections of a creative and universal God. Creative and universal He is, yet unique and individual He made us. Who is capable of holding all of God's attributes? No one. However, I see your differences and mine as a collaboration that portrays more of God to the world.

All of these facets of self-expression are just various *forms of communicating* what God has beautifully given to us to enhance our communication of who we are—it makes all our creative forces behind what we write, make, compose, and design a *divine* work. If it weren't for someone's natural proclivity for science, we may not have modern medicine. If it weren't for someone's natural tendency to educate, we may not have teachers. If it weren't for someone's natural inclination toward figuring out why things work, we may not have cars, or phones, or cameras. Who you are and what you naturally express and value is important.

This matters because this understanding provides ultimate security and completely frees you to be exactly who you are. It reminds you *why* you have the set preferences and gifts you have and why the world needs them. The exact space you inhabit on Earth is a part of His design. Whether you wear chic monochromatic clothes instead of sparkly rainbow sequins, or whether you listen to classical violin rather than the country fiddle, or whether you prefer minimalist Scandinavian design over an explosion of stuff, what you love and how you express your individuality is important. Without you, we lose certain elements that are needed in a world that desperately needs *you*— every little exceptional and unique part of you.

12

THE SERIOUS BUSINESS OF FUN

YOU KNOW YOU LIKE IT

Nineties pop was blaring out of my iPhone, which was strategically balanced between the hot and cold knobs on my sink. The bathroom looked like a mad scientist's lab with sticks of eyeliner and brushes of every size and shape and color, multiple lipstick tubes with lids off, and blush palettes open. As I leaned toward the mirror to ever-so-carefully apply my mascara, I glanced down at my daughter, who was standing at my feet, little hands reaching over the counter and picking up item after item. As careful as she was trying to be, her little hands and two-year-old unawareness—coupled with the fragile palettes and soft brushes in my beautifully lined-up rows of makeup—was basically like King Kong tearing through Manhattan.

"Jules, think you can be ready in five minutes?" I heard my husband ask from behind me.

"Yeah, totally! I just need to get dressed. Can you take Blaise for me? She's terrorizing my makeup."

"Sure," he responded graciously as he picked her up and took her into the kitchen to wash her hands before dinner.

You see, tonight was not just any night. It was a special night. It was date night. And my goodness, we *love* date night. My hubby and I adore hanging out with each other. For about four to six blissful hours it's just me looking at him and him looking at me. I love our conversation, our laughs (not to mention a nice plate of steak and a good glass of wine). I'm not the type of gal who cries when she leaves her babies at home with a sitter for the night. Benny has always been my favorite person to hang out with and this night was no exception—but I was running behind.

Ten minutes passed, and I heard him yell from downstairs, "Babe, are you about ready? The car is here."

This is always a problem for me. I am always running late and *he* knows that. He is often annoyed with my lack of punctuality and *I* know that. This doesn't mean I necessarily take this mutual understanding as license to never try to be on time, but it *does* mean that we have both become aware that this issue will be something we will most likely always wrestle with (unless God sees fit to give me an internal clock).

At this point he was standing in the doorway and saw

that I was regrettably still in my robe and nowhere near dressed. "Jules, I'm going to have to call the restaurant. We're already late."

I pulled my leather skirt on and as soon as I started to button it, I pulled it right back off. *Not what I want to wear,* I thought to myself. I realized that my Benny was probably pulling his beard hair out by now. Suddenly I saw the figurative relational fork in the road right in front of us: We can either have a great night or a crappy one. That's when I decided to take some drastic measures.

I threw my robe on the floor to reveal my birthday suit. I quickly turned to face my hubby and gave him a big hug, squeezed his butt, wrapped one arm around his waist, and grabbed his hand as if to begin a ballroom dance as I not-so-gracefully swayed his massive 210-pound body in my arms. Then I stopped and looked him in the eyes, stuck my finger up my nose, and said, "Oh, babes. I know I'm annoying and I'm sorry I'm late...but you know you like it." I stepped back and shot him a flirtatious wink.

He laughed and threw his hands up in surrender. The ice that had been building up began to crack, and once again, true love thawed our frozen walk-in closet. He tossed me a dress, giving me a look as if to say, *Just wear this; it's coming off later anyhow.* I laughed, put the dress on, and we were out the door.

THE MARRIAGE LITMUS TEST

People ask me a lot how Ben and I have maintained such a fun relationship (I mean, we're basically obsessed with each other). The quick answer is: We flirt. *A lot*. Sure, flirting is not the apple a day that will keep the doctor away, but it certainly works as a good litmus test.

If Ben and I don't want to grab each other's butts, laugh while whispering something inappropriate in the other's ear, or kiss a little longer than necessary, I know something is off—with either me or him.

Flirtation is a sign of security in marriage. It's the "just because," the "no strings attached," the "I like you because I like you" message that seems to be lacking in so many relationships. Marriages have gone from pure enjoyment and a let's-do-life-together mentality to a just-don't-cheat-and-just-stay-together mentality—and that's just no fun.

Think back to your dating days—or maybe you're in those days right now (and if so, go get 'em, tiger). Flirtation is used all the time to playfully express your interest in someone. Sure, sometimes flirtation in a new dating relationship can feel somewhat contrived and it can feel risky because you don't know how it will be received. Flirtation in a new relationship is more about trying to figure out how he or she feels about you and less about the other person. *Will he think I'm cute if I playfully bump into him while we're walking? Will she think I'm funny and laugh if I tickle her when we hug?* Flirtation is fun and necessary for attraction as you are getting to know someone, but at this stage it is not a reflection of your commitment to each other. *Sure, he doesn't need me, but does he even want me?* The existence of flirtation may answer the more basic questions, but it barely grazes the surface about how truly secure you both feel with each other at this point.

In marriage, however, flirtation isn't *needed* to catch the fly with honey (you've already done that), but it can demonstrate something that often gets lost post "I do." With all the serious business that comes with walking through life together—with all the needs like financial, spiritual, and parental stability—silly flirtation can remind you of the *want*. The actual desire of *wanting* to be around this human being that you've committed your life to.

So let's fast-forward a bit—you've dated a few years, you've fallen in love, he's put a ring on your finger, you've walked down the aisle—you are secure and committed.

It's a rainy Monday morning. The new house you bought as newlyweds has lost its luster and is peppered with plastic trucks and wooden blocks from the little one. You are both running late to work because the dog left you a good-morning present on the rug and little Billy didn't want to brush his teeth that morning. You haven't even been able to make it down the stairs for your coffee, but when you finally do, you discover that the Mr. Coffee is on the fritz again. You had asked your husband to take a look at it or pick out a new one, but of course he hasn't yet. You turn to find the trash can overflowing with the weekend's remains and the dishwasher full of dirty dishes just like every Monday morning.

Your car is parked behind his car and he walks up behind you while your head is stuck in the inner workings of the coffee maker's mechanics and tickles your waist while playfully whispering into your neck, "Excuse me, ma'am. Mind getting out of my way?"

Now, if you were to check your mental priority list, you would (hopefully) see your spouse at the top of that list and a busted coffee maker that simply needs replacing slightly lower. Sure, un-potty-trained animals, busted appliances, dirty dishes, cranky children, and trash are not the glamorous parts of marriage, but they are to be expected. You can let them dictate your marriage or you can let your marriage dictate them. That figurative relational fork in the road makes itself known again and you see two options:

- Option number one: Chew him out for being a lazy, thoughtless partner and walk out the door leaving him anxious and Billy without a ride to day care.

- Option number two: Turn around and say, "Um, sir, you're just going to have to wait until I'm good and ready," slapping him on the butt as you walk away. As you head out the door with Billy in tow, you turn to your husband and say, "Hey, hun, do you think we can talk about some things later?" When you get to work, you get on Amazon and get that new coffee maker shipped for an overnight delivery.

Now, option number one definitely happens sometimes and that's okay. Ladies and gents, we've got to be gentle with ourselves. When you know that, yes, you do love your spouse and that, yes, they are worth apologizing to later and being candid with, then you can have an open and honest discussion about what frustrates you and why those little things stress you out (especially on Mondays). We all know that sometimes the overwhelming amount of stress in other facets of life slips through the cracks and take forms in smaller, less important things. (Remember emotional laziness?) However, the option you pick can be a good indicator of the current condition of how you are prioritizing both your marriage and yourself.

Here's the thing about flirting as a litmus test. What is the first thing that goes out of a relationship when there's tension? It's the humor, the playfulness, the unnecessary physical touch that is replaced with "don't touch me" unspoken words that are louder than anything you could say through a megaphone. If you're pissed at your husband because of something he did or did not do, the icy look you give him when he tries to grab your butt is your nonverbal cue that something is off. Husbands and wives, when your flirting is met with annoyance, don't shut down. This is a tactic from the dark ages begging for a conversation. Flirtation met with resistance = let's talk.

Time and time again, I have seen people fall out of love because the flirtation and friendship are lost in their marriage. To call your husband or wife a friend is to say you enjoy being with them and you are comfortable in their presence. To flirt with your husband or wife is to say you find them attractive and genuinely want them. Maintaining a spirit of flirtation and friendship in a marriage is key.

Ben and I did not decide to get married because we needed anything from the other person. Neither of us was trying to fill some void in the other person. We got married because we were best friends and we genuinely loved hanging out every day. I somehow felt *more* myself when I was around him. Which is why when I give advice to girls asking me, "How do I know if he's the guy for me?" my answer is simple and uncomplicated: "Who do you want to hang out with all the time?" Obviously, there is more to it than that—the whole parental approval thing, spiritual compatibility, and real-life logistics are pretty important too.

Of course, it is important to find the right person for you—but do you consider *yourself* to be the right person? Do you know what you believe in enough to express who you are to another person confidently? Do you find *yourself* worth spending an entire life with? The same qualities you search for apply to you too. The more you know yourself, the more you'll know what to look for in another person. If you do not know yourself and are not okay with yourself, absolutely no relationship will complete you, because you're never going to find a relationship that will make you more okay with yourself or God. At the end of the day, you are still going to be you and the person you're in a relationship with will still just be the person you're in a relationship with.

The point? For relationships to be filled with joy and fun and excitement (and be healthy, for that matter), there *must* be security, and that security must be found within yourself. You've got to be okay with yourself first before you're ever going to be okay with anyone else.

The security of a relationship is contingent upon how secure each of the individuals are in themselves—both in who they are and in God, because security in a relationship is only as secure as the individuals are.

MUCK 'N' ALL

The muck. The dirt. The stuff we try and hide. The stuff we like to pretend isn't there. The bad stuff. The baggage. The hurt from the past. The annoying tendencies. The propensity to be late. The tics. The quirks.

If you're a living, breathing human being, you've got muck, which means when you are in a relationship, be it a friendship or an intimate one, there will be muck.

So, are we all mucked? Is the opportunity for any healthy relationship totally mucked? Nope. Oddly enough, it is the exposure of the muck that allows for a relationship to be healthy and happy. It is the recognition of it, the awareness of it, the forgiveness of it, and even the expectation of it that allows our muck to not muck up every relationship.

When you have security in yourself, that is the appropriate breeding ground necessary for honesty, transparency, and vulnerability to grow in a relationship. Security in yourself before God is why you are able to see your own muck, sometimes make fun of it, apologize for it when it hurts others, and move on. Security in yourself before God is what will allow you to see the muck of your friend or your spouse and see it as a part of life and not the straw that breaks the camel's back.

Actually, being aware of all the muck is what it means to be lighthearted. When you think of a lighthearted person, what do you think of? Someone who is anxious and always taking things personally or blowing little things out of proportion? No! A light heart is, well, light. It is not burdened. A light heart is not ignorant of the muck but is able to see it and respond to it appropriately. A light heart doesn't expect friends or a spouse to be muck-free and perfect. A light heart knows there is muck in him or her, and when it shows, it is gracious. A light heart does not expect her own heart to be muck-free. She is aware of her muck. She is aware her muck sucks but recognizes that this is the tension we live in. Sinner and saint— somewhere between Jesus and 2Pac.

Muck is inevitable. Hurt is inevitable. But when people hurt each other, if their hearts can get back to a soft place, a hurt relationship can be restored. The problem is that when people hurt each other, they often seek to protect themselves from further wounds by hardening their hearts and making them heavy. Of course, *hurt* is an extremely broad word to use and no, not all hurt is equal, nor does it need to be treated equally, but my main point here is that security in relationships is directly correlated to our hearts remaining soft, open, and light.

A heavy, hardened heart carries around lots of boxes and bags and containers for all the muck to live in. It hides it with heavy iron walls so that no one can see it and it will never be known. But security in oneself and in God looks like this: taking all the baggage, putting it out on the table, and allowing people to see all the mucky imperfections. It can take years and years of looking at and digging through, but eventually you find people—good people like a loving husband and trusted friends—to sift through all that muck with you and unpack some of that baggage you might have been carrying around. Because when you start sifting through, it is when you really start to understand what to give a muck about. You start to keep that mental priority list in the forefront of your brain and choose to always put your own husband above broken appliances and the expectation that everything is always going to be comfortable and happy and clean.

This is the security that results in a beautiful, fun, flirtatious, lighthearted marriage—the realization of your own muck and your spouse's muck, and the decision to love yourself and others anyway, muck 'n' all.

FREEDOM FOR FUN

My middle name is Joy, so I think my parents must have somehow infused in me the need for fun. However, as I've grown older, I've begun to feel that this little thing called "fun" is being constantly challenged and devalued. The scowling eye of the mature, the snarky snuff of the holy people, the annoyed frustration of the intellectuals. *Fun? Who needs fun? We need more seriousness, more maturity, and more time for study.*

Now, I do understand where the "fun is not mature" point of view is coming from. As you get older, consequences go from getting put in a time-out to losing a job, or bad decisions that used to result in having a toy taken away might now result in losing your house. Reality of life is weighty. Reality of struggle is weighty. The reality of parenting is weighty. The reality of sickness and death is weighty. So, when these weighty real-life situations are ignored or when "fun" is used as a mere Band-Aid, it can feel trite and ignorant.

However, do you remember in chapter 8 when we talked about the word *telos*, meaning "whole"? When we live wholly, we are living in the understanding that we are imperfect humans living in an imperfect world with a bent toward perfection and the divine. We aren't avoiding the bad, but we also aren't avoiding the good. This is what it means to live whole.

So where does fun come into play when we talk about living whole? Fun can be the aftermath of wholeness. Fun happens when you take the whole entire picture of a situation, including whatever struggle you are feeling or tension you are experiencing, and filter it through your heart authority's belief that you are loved and you are wanted, and that pain is for your growth. Once that reality is known, the fun starts. It's a holistic response to the security you feel in your heart, that you are loved and that whatever you are doing is *worth* doing, or whatever you are going through is *worth* pressing on and pressing through—whether it be fun through self-expression, your work, or your relationships.

Look, I get it. Relationships are hard. But they are also beautiful. Relationships—in marriage or friendships—are life-giving and cause us to grow. However, we only grow when we take all the good, the bad, and the mucky and lay it all out on the table of perspective and decide that, yes, this relationship is *worth it*. This relationship is *worth* the effort it takes to maintain the fun. Because, at the end of the day, we remember the laughs we've shared, the trips we've taken, the shared smiles.

Fun, however elementary it may seem from a distance, is profound. It's proof of confidence and security. It's a re-alization of proper prioritization—that family and friends are more important than the little stuff that tends to trip us up. Maybe it's just me, but I have definitely missed out on the fun at parties when I spent the whole night over-thinking something someone said or obsessing about the fact that I got invited weeks after her so what does that say about me.

It reminds me of the time my sister had her feelings hurt by a conversation she overheard my brother having with my other sister when we were younger. She sat there and listened, sentence by sentence, becoming more and more offended and hurt by what they were saying about her. When she left the room in a pool of tears, my dad went to find her.

"Sugar, what's wrong?" he asked her.

As she wept, she recounted what her cruel siblings were saying about her. After a minute of listening, my dad interrupted her.

"Sugar, they weren't talking about *you*. They were talking about a book."

We all had a good laugh about it later, and when the dust of emotions settled and all was right in the Gilmore household again, I will never forget someone saying sarcastically, "Lizzy, you know when we are watching the Super Bowl on TV and all the players huddle together on the field? Do you think they're talking about you then too?" There is much truth in jest, because, I hate to break it to you, the most insecure people I know are also the people who think everything is either about them or is in some way affecting them. It may come as a shock, but the party is definitely not about the order in which all the partyers were invited. Chances are no one has kept close enough tabs. However, people will remember the crazy, fun dancing.

Secure people, on the other hand (which my sister Lizzy most definitely exemplifies in the most glorious way now), are confident in who they are and what they believe. They are unapologetic. Secure people are actually *free* to have fun, because (1) the world is *not* about us, (2) we do not know it all, (3) our kids spilling milk is honestly not something to get upset about, (4) running late for a date is not grounds for marital strife, and (5) what so-and-so said in frustration is about them, not you.

There is so much that you can tell about a person by whether or not they are able to have fun in life.

If you can look at life and situations through a *telos* lens, then you can consider and address the things that *are* about you. The things that hurt, you recognize and deal with. The things that really aren't about you at all, well, we let those go. And the result of that? Security— and that security frees us to have fun. Crazy ballroom dancing, late-night laughing, Crayola-colors-wearing, butt-squeezing and all.

13
WORTHWHILENESS

THE PARTICULARLY WILD WILDFLOWER

Once upon a time, in a sprawling field that rested quietly below a pink, endless spring sky, there grew a cluster of wildflowers. Each unique in their shape, shade, and scent, the cluster of wildflowers smiled and admired each other's differences. Together they would close and open their petals as the sun rose and fell each morning and night.

However, there was one wildflower that was *particularly* wild, swaying back and forth, fluffing her soft petals proudly and straightening her strong stem just as straight as she possibly could. And though she was a particularly wild wildflower, she was content and at peace and full of joy to be exactly where she was, in her sprawling field, next to the rest of the cluster. She felt brave, confident, and brilliant.

One day as this particularly wild wildflower was dancing in the unmoving air, she heard the voice of another
flower that was planted in a perfectly lovely garden only
feet away—but she had never noticed it before, as she
had always faced the opposite direction. *Don't you know
that you're just a weed? Nobody likes weeds. They are
ugly and accidental. You should have been a petunia
like me.* Despite one of her petals wilting, the particularly
wild wildflower straightened her stem tall and proud.

Suddenly, a gust of chilled breeze whipped behind the
cluster of wildflowers and caused the grasses that grew
between them to shift. Suddenly the particularly wild
wildflower was struck by the whip of a beautiful and vi-
cious thorn bush. She straightened her strong stem and
fluffed her soft petals in pride and defense.

But as weeks passed and the words of the petunia and
the thorn of the rose pierced, she no longer had the desire to move with the warm wind, or to straighten her
scratched stem, or to fluff her wilting petals. Ashamed of
her scars and her appearance, she no longer believed herself to be the brave, confident, and brilliant particularly
wild wildflower that she was.

The particularly wild wildflower gradually felt less and
less comfortable. Every day felt like a hopeless attempt
at hiding scars, so she would laugh and smile to hide
the fear. She became reclusive in her own mind, bitter at
the beauty in the uniqueness and seeming imperfection
of the other wildflowers and the flowers in the nearby
garden.

One day, as the particularly wild wildflower stared at the endless pink sky, she saw something in the distance that she had never seen before. Closer and closer the figure came, cutting through the familiar landscape. The particularly wild wildflower saw a towering creature that exuded radiance and whimsy and fearlessness and purity...things that the wildflower once saw in her wild self.

As the creature got closer, it slowed and bent toward the earth. Reaching out from her sides like two branches out of the trunk of a majestic tree, she picked one, two, three wildflowers. The particularly wild wildflower gasped. Perhaps she could be chosen by this magnificent creature. Fluffing her wilted petals as much as she could, she began to straighten her stem. But looking down, she saw them— the scars on her stem—a permanent reminder of the particularly wild wildflower's imperfections.

Not a moment later, the particularly wild wildflower felt a gentle touch. The magnificent creature began to dig in a circle around her. The particularly wild wildflower felt a wave of shame and embarrassment and began to argue with the creature: *"I am not beautiful enough. I am only a weed. I am too flawed and too hurt. There are so many other wildflowers and petunias and roses here that seem to have no scars... See the others you are holding now! Please let me stay where I belong, among the tall grass. I think I am quite happy right where I have been."*

The creature just smiled down upon her and slowly and gently, with great care and great intention, lifted the particularly wild wildflower out of the dirt. Warmed by the embrace of the very tall creature, the little wildflower felt safe for the first time in a great while.

The creature began to move over the field gracefully, still holding the particularly wild wildflower. The wildflower wondered where she was headed, what she would do, and why she was chosen. As if her thoughts could be heard, the majestic creature spoke: *"You were chosen because you are mine. You have always been my particularly wild wildflower. I will make you brave, confident, and brilliant again. You are worthy because I have decided you are."*

As the creature slowed her pace, the particularly wild wildflower looked around to realize she was part of a bouquet, a bouquet of very particular wildflowers. Every wildflower was a different shape and shade and scent. And up close, she could see that every wildflower was just like her—imperfect. Stems marked by history, a broken leaf, a misshapen petal. Was it possible that the creature did not care that they were imperfect? Could it be that perhaps the creature wanted it that way?

The particularly wild wildflower began to feel something new. A stem-shivering sensation that began at the base of her root and moved all the way up through her leaves and through her petals: worthiness. This feeling of worthiness flamed with fury like wildfire through her again and again. Courage and confidence and brilliance. She straightened her stem, suddenly believing that she was part of something grand, something uncharted, something divine. Then slowly, very slowly, to the rhythm of some distant melody, the particularly wild wildflower looked ahead and realized the majestic creature was walking in the tall grass, graceful step by graceful step, to her groom.

A WEED'S WORTH

You were planted on this earth. You, too, are a wildflower, and goodness knows that *no one* can tame you. Sure, people can stomp on you and mow over you and treat you as if you are not a flower but a weed. People will try to control you. They will try to fence you in with their cultural expectations and they will try to spray you with Weed-B-Gon and God-shame and manipulation. Thorns will come along and try to pin you down with trends and the newest way to "be cool."

When the heavy rain rolls in, you may feel like you're going to drown, but what will you do with that rain? You will *use* it. You will soak it in. You will be empowered by it. You won't let the rain win. It will become one of the most amazing and redemptive things in your life, because it is what will make you grow.

When the sun comes out and it gets hot and you feel like you're drying up, you will dig deeper and deeper into the ground. Your foundation will grow firmer, and in turn, you will find the water—the living water that God offers us in His Word, and from that you will be nourished.

When the wind shifts and new ideas blow your way, you will not be swayed. Because you are grounded in what you know to be true. And when another breeze blows and it is confirmed as truth, you will sway and dance in that breeze.

Have you ever seen those bright yellow flowers that rule the entire world and sometimes turn to fluffy white clouds of seed? They give boring manicured lawns pops of yellow—like splatters of vibrant paint. Dandelions. That is you. That is me. You've been planted and will never stop growing. You cannot be stopped and you will never be able to be fenced in or cut down. Your bright and bruised yellow petals and your strong and scratched stem will never be tamed, because you, my friend, are a freaking wildflower—and not just any wildflower, but a particularly wild wildflower.

Which means you are *worth* it. You were planted into the ground by God, and you will know this because no one will ever be able to be rid of you. You are a dandelion that was created not to be controlled and manipulated by others, but to relish in the purpose that God has given you and be a part of the incredibly vibrant bouquet He has planned for you.

REDEMPTIVE THINKING

I've been called a positive thinker a lot and, to be honest, it always kind of annoys me. Of course, it is always well meaning—positivity is just about as trendy and smiled upon as kale—but it never rings true for me.

You see, positivity is only half the story. Perhaps we can chalk it up to semantics and word choice, but I tend to think of positive thinkers and negative thinkers in the same way—extremists and masters at avoidance.

When someone shares that they have just found out they have lost their job, the positive thinker responds, "Stay positive! God has a plan!" This response can come off as avoidance of the reality and the weight of the situation. Obviously, yes, God has a plan, but a "too-positive" response can feel trite and not genuine. Truth is hard to swallow sometimes, and the defense mechanism against having to deal with anything hard or painful is to run from the hard stuff with a smile on your face and a sometimes-unrealistic perspective.

Likewise, negative thinkers attach themselves to only one end of reality: the negative. They use cynicism, sarcasm, and negativity as a defense mechanism. If everything is doomed anyhow, then why invest? Negative thinkers may think, *Well, if you show up to work as late as you show up to dinner, then it's no wonder you got fired!* While this may be true, it is not helpful and it is certainly not a kind response. Negative thinkers love to think they know it all. The negative thinker avoids the possibility of pain by attaching themselves to the unconstructive. When you get to be everyone else's know-it-all doctor, then you don't have to deal with your own crap or pain or suffering. You can find solace and avoid reality through an I-knew-it-all-along-so-what's-the-point? mentality.

Forget the positive and negative; I want to be a *redemptive* thinker. Redemptive thinking redeems the way we ordinarily misjudge the world. Redemptive thinking tries to see it all and avoid nothing. Positive and negative thinking take one piece of the pie, while redemptive thinking sees not only the pie in its entirety, but also the process that went into making the whole pie. It sees a story. It sees every ingredient—each grain of flour and each seed that became a cherry—on a journey of becoming its ultimate aim, a delicious Dutch cherry pie.

Redemptive thinking is the best kind of storytelling. It sees everything as full of purpose—it sees pain as a solemn opportunity for growth and change. It looks at every aspect of life as a part of a bigger narrative moving to a profound conclusion that is too complex to chalk up to two opposite ends of the spectrum.

Our experiences are constantly shifting, and redemptive thinking is how we can make sense of them. By taking the disparate fragments of our lives and placing them together in big-picture story form, we create a unified whole that allows us to understand our lives as coherent. This idea that every single piece of the mosaic has importance—that every torn petal of the wildflower and each flower in the bouquet is needed—is a key source of understanding that life itself is indeed meaningful.

Because we are a collection of all these moments, it means that we, too, are meaningful. Just like moments can't be watered down to simply positive and negative, we as human beings can't be simplified to being "good" or "bad."

Similarly, I don't believe that God can be boiled down to simply being a positive or negative thinker. He is not a God who sits up on His pink gumball throne surrounded by cotton candy clouds, just delightfully awaiting the next blissfully ignorant pawn to wisp on up to heaven inside her shiny translucent bubble of laughter.

He is also not a God who sits up on His fiery throne, scowl on His face, impatiently awaiting the next judgmental, self-righteous negative pawn to grind their way up to heaven by the sweat of their brow and the rest of humankind's sins.

No way. Our God has a heart for the bigger picture. He is a God who saves and regains us from the broken world. He is a God who allows us to grow from our pain, to learn from our mistakes, and to change and flourish into a work of art that can bring hope amidst chaos. Our God is defined by His constant redemption. And this redemption story is *key* to understanding your worth and the unique story that you are telling. Because, sorry, you don't even get to decide your worth. You are like a tube of minty fresh toothpaste. Sure, you can argue and complain that you don't deserve your $4.49 value, but your arguing will not change the reality of what you are worth. That's decided by the creator: Colgate. (Yes, I just compared all of mankind to toothpaste...just making sure you've grown some thick skin by now.) Likewise, your inherent worth was decided by your Creator. No one gets to decide that.

He does. He decided, by creating you, that you are so incredibly worthwhile. Like the flowers in the field, your very existence on this earth determines your worth. God has given every single one of us implicit value because He created us for His glory.

You are worth it to Him, because only things worthwhile are worth redeeming. And guess what? Christ's death upon the cross (and resurrection) confirmed that redemption for the world. When you realize that God Himself has claimed you as worthy, because He chose willingly to sacrifice His son, you are secure. The best part is that security breeds joy, freedom, purpose, and acceptance both of yourself and of others.

Sure, some of you might be thinking, *Well, geez, Jules, this all sounds like positive thinking to me!*

Nope. We've all been dealt different cards in this poker game of life. Suffering is a very real thing. As we know, even the most perfect human had to suffer at the cross so that universal redemption could happen. You get no say in whether you get a royal flush or fall flat, but either way, you get to decide what you will do with the cards you have been dealt. This is not just positive or negative. This is redemptive.

A redemptive story is a story line of both the positive *and* the negative. It's seeing everything with eyes wide open. It's looking at the cards you've been dealt and seeing that they are not all aces, but they are also not all jokers. It's asking yourself: *What am I going to do with what I have been given?*

Some more good news? Knowing your worth *does* give you a leg up. It sees that all the cards were dealt with a bigger purpose in mind. Because fortunately our God is not out to win. He is not the Bellagio and you the naïve gambler. If we are in pain or mess up, He redeems us—but we can only see it when we look through the lens of our inherent worth.

We will never see ourselves as redeemable until we see ourselves as worth redeeming. Therefore, if we don't see our marriage as worth it, then we will not put forth the necessary energy and fight to make it more than just okay. If we don't see our children as worth it, we won't put forth the necessary work to train them and help them learn how to be hard workers and kind human beings. If we don't see ourselves as worth it, we won't put forth the work to know ourselves and challenge our thinking and grow like the scrappy wildflowers we are.

A DANDELION'S PURPOSE

God could have created dandelions merely as little yellow jagged flowers that pop up in yards unexpectedly. He could have simply made some people to love them and some people to hate them. He could have left it at that. But He didn't. No matter what side you take in the battle of the dandelions, there is something that is true and will not change. These weedy wildflowers are chock-full of purpose.

Besides granting childhood wishes since the beginning of time, every single part of the dandelion plant—from the roots to the leaves—can be used to benefit the human body. God created these seemingly unwanted flowers to provide relief from liver disorders, diabetes, urinary disorders, skin problems, jaundice, anemia, and even cancer!

No matter what people do to the dandelion—whether they mow it down or try to uproot it—the dandelion's worth and purpose do not change. God created it for bigger things, whether it's to cure a disease or make a bouquet more beautiful or bring joy to a wishful-thinking toddler.

And sure, not everyone will know the dandelion's secret worth and not every flower will play the same role, but the best part is that we are ultimately unified by the fact that our worth is implicit and our own unique purpose and presence is important. We will each be gathered. Every single wildflower on every single sprawling hill and every single meadow will be held to the chest of Christ and carried as the largest, most diverse bouquet the world has ever known. Because what is a bouquet without diversity? We are to be unified, not uniform. This is a collaboration—a collective conglomeration of all the unique and broken and tattered and different and beautiful and not-so-beautiful-but-all-so-very-worthy wildflowers—not a competition.

Can you imagine Chopin writing a composition that consisted of one note? He would not be the renowned composer we know him to be if that were the case. He would be laughed off the stage if he performed a piece composed of only D#s. B.O.R.I.N.G.

So, stop wishing you were an A when you're a D#. Stop telling middle C that she's not as deep and grounded as lower C. Stop telling the high G to hurry up and not be so high pitched. She's a high G. She was planted on the keyboard of life to play that part. So, shut up about it and own your D#. Be the best D# you can possibly be. The most in-tune, expressive, ringing, dancing, beautiful D# you have ever been. You are worth it.

But all the while, remember that a variety of notes is what makes a song. A variety of wildflowers is what makes a bouquet. The good and the bad, together, make for redemption.

Here's the thing about music and flowers and the redemptive story that we are a part of—they all *need* diversity. The possibility to thrive is dependent on variation. Success demands collaboration.

That is why you are you, and I am me—because the world needs us. The world needs *you*. The world needs your color, your brilliance, your resilience, your self-expression, your variation, and your difference. The world needs to see your scratched stem and broken petals. Why? Because we are all imperfect and we are all in this together—and only when we are together, unified but not uniform, are we able to play the magnificent masterpiece God has orchestrated. Because we are all worth it.

This is why we put down our phones and pick up a book instead. Because investing in our minds is worth the time. This is why we take a deep breath and tie up the laces on our tennis shoes and walk into the gym for the first time since the baby was born. Because investing in our bodies to be strong and healthy is worth it. This is why we shoot our husband a wink even when the day has been rough, because making your marriage more than just "okay" is worth energy. This is why we ask questions about what we believe. Because ensuring that our faith is rooted in truth and not just the new passing trend is worth it. This is why we risk looking like a fool and step out on-stage to sing and dance with all of our hearts. Because doing what we love, even if we're not the best, is worth it. This is why we go back to school to get our degree. Because accomplishing great tasks is worth it. This is why we don't let the world *should* on us. Because walking in confidence before God in what He asks of us is worth it. This is why we fill our lives with beauty and meaning and purpose.

Come to grips with your worthwhileness and you will begin to step out in courage and confidence and brilliance!

ACKNOWLEDGMENTS

BEN, for being you. The kind, steady, old-school soul that strives for greatness in all things. You are everything to me. I want no one else. It has been my greatest joy to grow and change alongside you. Thank you for championing our love. #ArmyOfLovers

ZION, for opening my heart to a different kind of love. You constantly prove to me that we don't have to grow up to be used by God. You are perfectly intended for today. Also, thank you for teaching me the value of play!

KRUSE, for teaching me that cartwheels are an appropriate method of transportation. Also for the vivacious way you love me. I am the luckiest of moms.

BLAISE, for making me believe that I can hold you on my hip and press into my gifts at the same time. I hope you know I will always choose you.

* * *

DAD, I will always be your "hey, sugar" and you will always be my hero. Thank you for your unconditional love . . . I have always known I am safe with you.

MOM, you have empowered me to be who I am. You have served me and my family unceasingly and "thank you" does not feel adequate...so, one of these days I will get you to run for president.

MY SISTERS AND BROTHERS, for giving me a greater picture of who God is by knowing you and your families. You each display a different part of His character, His attributes, and His image. We are a unique and beautiful collaboration of different personalities, convictions, proclivities, and passions. I love us. We prove #UnityNotUniformity.

THE X. You know who you are, and this is all your fault. 'Cause, you see, you all have never let me quit. You've never ignored my texts. You have seen me at my worst and loved me anyway. You have listened to my rants and listened patiently. You have told me I am wrong when I am. You have reminded me of who I am when I have forgotten. You have listened to the concepts of this book a hundred million times and have never gotten annoyed but have always offered your insight. You have proven to me that true friendship is a rarity and a great treasure to find. Thank you for the largest Veuve known to human existence. Thank you for loving me, muck 'n' all.

* * *

LESLEY, for believing in me since the first day we met. You have always been pushing me to places I may not feel ready for, but you make me believe that I can, and you cheer me on the entire way. (It's always been steak and wine with you.)

LAUREN, for your appreciation of art in every form. You see others' stories as masterpieces that deserve the utmost respect and observance and I have been the fortunate recipient of that. Only by your coaching, direction, and willingness to get elbow-deep in my mind did this book become what it is.

ESTHER, for your drive and conviction. I will never forget our dinner in New York when you decided to begin celebrating before there was actually anything to celebrate...you taught me that the journey and the process is really what it's all about. Thank you for always being in my corner.

WHITNEY, for your honesty and spirit. I have never met a girl who speaks so much truth so sweetly. When you talk, I listen (and that's saying a lot).

LISA, for your confidence and hard work. That is the way to my heart. 'Nuff said.

HACHETTE—Keren, Patsy, and everyone on the team! For taking a chance on me in a big way. The first time we met in New York, I knew I could entrust this message to you. Thank you for asking questions, for editing my excess, and for giving me the creative freedom to thrive within.

OCTAGON ENTERTAINMENT—Kyell, Puraj, Chaya, and the whole team! For your commitment to excellence, your vision, and most of all, for encouraging vulnerability and community.

The cover shoot was a dream experience for me. Ikram,

for your eye, your commitment to it, and the kindness you have shown me. Adam Cohen, for your ability to capture humor, vulnerability, and all of the complexities that make me human. Andrew Colvin and the Anthony Cristiano team, for your gift at elevating beauty and your kind spirit.

* * *

ALL THE COLOR KIDS, for following my story, for reading this book, and for your constant source of inspiration. Since I began speaking on this subject and you began showing up to my shows, I started putting countless hours into this topic...but at the end of the day, it is your stories and your encouragement that have kept me going. This book is for you!

Love and Peace

Jules

NOTES

1. THE HEART AUTHORITY

1   Barbara Bonner, "The Many Faces of Courage," *Huffington Post* (November 2017). www.huffingtonpost.com/entry/the-many-faces-of-courage_us_5a1c1491e4b0bf1467a8482a.

2   "Moral Letters to Lucilius," *Encyclopædia Britannica*, Encyclopædia Britannica, Inc. www.britannica.com/topic/Moral-Letters-to-Lucilius.

3   http://www.telegraph.co.uk/news/science/science-news/7850263/Scientists-discover-secret-of-courage.html.

4   *Ernest Hemingway: Selected Letters 1917–1961* edited by Carlos Baker, pages 199–201.

5   Hana Hutchcroft, "Fearfully and Wonderfully Made," *Darling Magazine* (July 2015).

6   Michelle Bryner, "How Do Oysters Make Pearls?" LiveScience.com (November 2012). www.livescience.com/32289-how-do-oysters-make-pearls.html.

7   Ralph Waldo Emerson, "Nature." Gutenberg.com, Project Gutenberg (July 2009). www.gutenberg.org/files/29433/29433-h/29433-h.htm.

2. DON'T SHOULD ON ME

1   Kendra Cherry, "The False Consensus Effect: Why We Think Others Are Just Like Us," *Verywell* (June 2017).

2   https://www.simplypsychology.org/asch-conformity.html.

3   http://www.laphamsquarterly.org/fashion/wearing-pants.

3. EMOTIONAL LAZINESS

1   John Piper, What the Psalms Do. excerpt from "Songs That Shape the Heart and Mind," Sermon. https://www.desiringgod.org/articles/what-the-psalms-do.

4. VERBAL GYMNASTICS

1   Arthur Schopenhauer's *Parerga und Paralipomena*, Volume II, Chapter XXXI, Section 396.

5. EYES WIDE OPEN

1   Daily Capital Journal, Quote Page 6, Column 3, Salem, Oregon (June 22, 1908). Newspapers_com.

6. THE IMAGE AND IDENTITY MIX-UP

1   https://www.merriam-webster.com/dictionary/image.
2   C. S. Lewis, "Mere Christianity," in *Mere Christianity* (Grand Rapids, MI: Zondervan, 2001), 158.

7. THE FIVE O'CLOCK GLASS OF PINOT

1   Enneagram Institute, "Type Two." www.enneagraminstitute.com/type-2/.

8. SPIRITUAL BOTOX

1   https://www.medicalnewstoday.com/articles/158647.php.
2   http://biblehub.com/greek/5056.html.

9. THE TENSION

1   C. S. Lewis, afterword to *The Pilgrim's Regress*, 3rd ed. (Grand Rapids, MI: Wm B Eerdmans, 2014), 204.

2   C. S. Lewis, "The Weight of Glory" in *The Essential C. S. Lewis* (New York: Scribner, 2017), 363.

3   http://study.com/academy/lesson/the-school-of-athens-by-raphael-description-figures-analysis.html.

4   Richard Baxter, "The Saints' Everlasting Rest; the Divine Life; and Dying Thoughts, Etc.," in *The Saints' Everlasting Rest; the Divine Life; and Dying Thoughts, Etc.* (London: Blackie and Son, 1842), 74.

10. THE UNINHIBITED LIFE

1   https://www.psychologytoday.com/files/attachments/34246/zabelina-robinson-2010a.pdf.

2   Gordon MacKenzie, *Orbiting the Giant Hairball* (New York: Viking Press, 1996), 20–22.

3   Robert Scott Root-Bernstein and Michelle Root-Bernstein, "Sparks of Genius: the Thirteen Thinking Tools of the World's Most Creative People," in *Sparks of Genius: the Thirteen Thinking Tools of the World's Most Creative People* (Boston: Houghton Mifflin Harcourt, 2001), 2.

4   American Society of Landscape Architects, "ASLA 2006 Student Awards." www.asla.org/awards/2006/studentawards/282.html.

11. THE COLOR KIDS

1   https://www.washingtonpost.com/news/style/wp/2014/10/14/gene-weingarten-setting-the-record-straight-on-the-joshua-bell-experiment/?utm_term=.d69e23d3e7c2.

2   Dr. Seuss, *The Sneetches: and Other Stories* (Collins, 1998).

ABOUT THE AUTHOR

Julianna Zobrist is a rural Iowa City girl, raised on classical music, Michael Jackson, and farm-grown corn. Since her recent record release of *Shatterproof*, Julianna has performed at numerous events and venues around the nation and has been featured by top media across the globe including *Forbes*, *Huffington Post*, CBS, FOX News, *Parade* magazine, and *Sports Illustrated* among others. Julianna divides her time between Nashville, Tennessee, and Chicago, Illinois, with her husband, Ben Zobrist, and her children, Zion, Kruse, and Blaise.